THE WORLD
ON
RED ALERT

DICK PERFECT

THE WORLD
ON
RED ALERT

**A responsibly presented Biblical
warning of the awesome events
predicted to be coming upon the
world for its continuing Christ
rejection and Godlessness.**

DICK PERFECT

Printed by E. L. Jones & Son, Cardigan, West Wales

THE WORLD

ON

RED ALERT

**IS NOW PUBLISHED
IN THE FOLLOWING LANGUAGES :**

Chichewa

English

French

Fulani

Hausa

Hindi

Igala

Kanuri

Malayalam

Nupe

Tamil

Telugu

Tiv

Yoruba

THE WORLD

ON

RED ALERT

70,000 COPIES IN PRINT
REVISED AND UPDATED 2002

ISBN 1 874 618 24 0

Bible text is reproduced from the Good
News Bible – American Bible Society,
New York, 1966, 1971 and 4th Edition 1976.
Published by the Bible Societies /
Harper Collins with permission.

Indian Publishers
River of Peace Publications
7/5 Anna Salai, Kodaikanal
Tamil Nadu, India

Nigerian Publishers
Christian Literature in
Nigerian Languages Project
29 Shendam Street
P.O. Box 1
Jos Plateau State
Nigeria

U.K. Publishers
Rhos-Llyn Christian Centre
Penparc, Cardigan
West Wales, SA43 2AB

"Come people of all nations!
Gather round and listen.
Let the whole earth and everyone
living on it come here and listen.
The Lord is angry with all the nations."

(Isa. 34. 1-2)

PREFACE

"The World On Red Alert" is a handbook, which sets out to show in compact form how literally the apocalyptic truths increasingly fit into a near future that now seems highly plausible.

Throughout history Bible prophets have brought advance information of God's intentions to those who will listen for: "The Sovereign Lord never does anything without revealing his plan to his servants, the prophets!" (Amos. 3.7.)

Back in the last half of the eight century BC God made a promise to Isaiah: "The things I predicted have now come true. Now I will tell you of new things even before they begin to happen." (Isa. 42: 9) A promise of God repeated centuries later when the Lord Jesus said of the Holy Spirit: "He will tell you of things to come." (John 16:13)

No doubt with this in mind, the apostle Peter says of the message proclaimed by the prophets: "You will do well to pay attention to it, because it is like a lamp shining in a dark place...for no prophetic message ever came just from the will of man, but, men were under the control of the Holy Spirit as they spoke the message that came from God." (2 Peter 1. 19-21)

May God bless you richly as you join with me in this very challenging, and at times disturbing study.

Dick Perfect

"The Lord has a case against the nations.
He will bring all people to trial
and put the wicked to death.
The Lord has spoken."

(Jer. 25.31)

Contents

All quotations taken from the Good News Bible,
unless stated otherwise.

"The Lord Almighty says that disaster
is coming on one nation after another,
and a great storm is gathering at the
far ends of the earth."

(Jer. 25: 32)

God's Red Alert

On the 14th May 1948, by restoring Israel to the status of a sovereign nation in her own land, God raised a long promised "Red Alert" signal flag: "The Lord will raise a signal flag to show the nations that he is gathering together again the scattered people of Israel and Judah and bringing them back from the four corners of the earth." (Isa. 11.12.)

God revealed to the prophet Hosea too that when the right time has come: "The people of Judah and the people of Israel will be reunited. They will choose for themselves a single leader, and once again they will grow and prosper in their land." (Hos. 1.11)

The Lord spoke also to the prophet Ezekiel saying: "take a wooden stick and write on it the words, 'The kingdom of Judah.' Then take another stick and write on it the words, 'The kingdom of Israel...' Hold in your hand the two sticks and let the people see them. Then tell them that I, the Sovereign Lord, am going to take all my people out of the nations where they have gone, gather them together, and bring them back to their own land. I will unite them into one nation in the land, on the mountains of Israel. They will have one king to rule over them, and they will no longer be divided into two nations or split into two kingdoms." Ezek. 37. 16-23)

Not since King Solomon's death in 931 B.C. had Israel and Judah been a single nation under one leader and living in their promised land. Then: "Solomon ruled in Jerusalem over all Israel for forty years [from 971 to 931 BC]. He died and was buried in David's City, and his son Rehoboam succeeded him as king." (2 Chron. 9. 30-31)

Then came division in the land, for: "the people of Israel rebelled, leaving Rehoboam as king only of the people who lived in the territory of Judah." (2 Chron.10 16-17) This was the southern part of the land occupied by the tribes of Judah and Benjamin.

A man named Jeroboam became king of the remaining ten tribes in the northern part of the land, just as God had promised him through the prophet Ahijah.

One day when Jeroboam had been out walking he saw the prophet Ahijah coming towards him. When they met "Ahijah took off the new robe he was wearing, tore it into twelve pieces, and said to Jeroboam, 'Take ten pieces for yourself, because the Lord the God of Israel says to you...'I will take the kingdom away from Solomon's son and will give you ten tribes.'" (1 Kings. 11. 30 & 35)

By 718 B.C. the kingdom of Israel in the north, and by 585 B.C. the kingdom of Judah in the south, had both become so rebellious against God that he carried out his long threatened punishment and scattered them amongst the nations of the world: "The Lord will scatter you like straw that is blown away by the desert wind. He has said that this will be your fate. This is what he has decided to do with you, because you have forgotten him and have trusted in false Gods." (Jer. 13. 24-25)

From then on until the 14th May 1948, when God raised his signal flag, the people of Israel and Judah had remained a scattered and divided nation, living for the most part out of their promised land.

Many fulfilled prophecies in Israel.

Since God raised his signal flag in 1948 re-establishing Israel as a nation, prophetic fulfilments have taken place one after another.

Many thousands of Israelis have since 1948 been allowed to leave Russia for Israel so fulfilling the prophecy: "The time is coming', says the Lord, 'when people will no longer swear by me as the living God who brought the people of Israel out of the land of Egypt. Instead they will swear by me as the living God who brought the people of Israel out of a northern land and out of all the other countries where I had scattered them." (Jer. 23: 7-8)

After 1948 the neglected and sparsely populated land began, again, very slowly at first, to grow crops in ever greater abundance. Today fruit and vegetables of extremely high quality not only provide for the rising population numbers, but have become important exports: "On the mountains of Israel the trees will again grow leaves and bear fruit for you, my people Israel...I am on your side, and I will make sure that your land is ploughed again and that seeds are sown there." (Ezek. 36: 8-9)

Another prophecy that began to be fulfilled soon after 1948, and has considerably increased in pace since then, is God's promise to His people: "You will live in the cities and rebuild everything that was left in ruins." (Ezek. 36: 10) Today Israel has large cities and towns with houses, hospitals, schools and factories, built to the highest specifications.

Increasing wealth, reflected in a high living standard, is also a fulfilled prophecy: "...I will make you more prosperous than ever." (Ezek. 36:11)

God's Plans not to be Frustrated

Probably most spectacular of all the prophecies currently being fulfilled is one so devastating that God himself describes it as "solemn", saying: "I, the Sovereign Lord, solemnly promise that the surrounding nations will be humiliated." (Ezek. 36:7)

Challenging God's authority is dangerous indeed, and likely to be very costly too.

In 1945, the Arab league declared that its member countries would unite in an attempt to frustrate the formation of a Jewish state in Palestine: "They (The Arab nations) are making secret plans... 'Come', they say, 'let us destroy their nation, so that Israel will be forgotten for ever." (Psalm 83: 3-4) So proclaiming a direct challenge to God who had promised the scattered Israelis:

"I will bring you, my people Israel, back to live again in the land. It will be your own land..." (Ezek. 36:12)

In 1948, Israel was declared a sovereign state, and recognised as such by the United Nations.

Totally disregarding this international proclamation however Egypt, Saudi Arabia, Lebanon, Jordan and Iraq immediately launched an unprovoked attack upon this tiny new state of no more than 650,000 Israelis. Amazingly the invaders were humiliated in defeat, and Israel substantially extended its borders. Thousands of Palestinian Arabs fled their homes as a result of this failed Arab aggression.

In 1967, Israel launched a powerful pre-emptive attack upon Egypt, Jordan and

Syria who had been receiving large supplies of Russian arms and technical support, and who, Israeli intelligence reported, were poised ready to attack Israel for a second time.

In the war that followed this Israeli strike the Arabs were again humiliated in the loss of Jerusalem, as well as significant areas of territory.

In 1973, while the Israelis were in their synagogues celebrating the Day of Atonement, Syria and Egypt launched a surprise attack. Within three weeks Israel had virtually defeated the attacking armies, and only the United Nations imposed cease-fire saved Syria and Egypt from even greater humiliation.

In 1980, Iraq attacked Iran and a long and fierce war ensued with heavy casualties on both sides. Poison gas was used by Iraq.

After the war, in an attempt to appease Iran, Iraq humiliated itself by returning to Iran the small area of land that had been captured during that costly war.

In 1990, Iraq invaded the Arab state of Kuwait, carrying out many atrocities against the Kuwaiti people. Saudi Arabia and Israel were also attacked with Iraqi missiles. After only 100 days, Iraq suffered a humiliating defeat by a United Nations Coalition Force.

When this war ended, a bitterly fought civil uprising ensued in Iraq with appalling atrocities leaving thousands more killed, maimed and starved to death.

Failed Peace Negotiations

Several attempts at reaching a peace agreement between the Palestinians and Israel have been made without success. During this time, Hamas, The Palestinian National Liberation Movement, and Hezbollah terrorist groups have carried out a series of incursions into Israel with murderous suicide bomb and gun attacks causing horrendous losses amongst the civilian population.

In the spring of 2002 in an attempt to defeat these suicide bombers and gunmen, Israel launched a fierce anti-terrorist search and destroy mission into the Palestinian townships and refuge camps.

Troubles in the Rest of the World.

Amongst nations, and within nations, wars and terrorism are mercilessly killing and maiming hundreds of thousands.

Poverty, sickness and drug addiction hasten millions to an early death, many without medical treatment of any kind.

Injustice, intolerance and persecution weigh heavily on millions of citizens living under oppressive regimes where religious martyrdom, forced labour and slave trading remain all too prevalent.

Warning to the Rich Nations.

Clearly however at this present time oppression, poverty and deprivation are not the lot of all countries. Some developed nations: "have piled up riches in these last days," and for many of their nationals "life here on earth" is "full of luxury and pleasure." To any of these affluent countries that might be accumulating wealth through exploitation of less developed populations God issues a solemn warning: "you rich people, listen to me! Weep and wail over the miseries that are coming upon you." (James 5. 1-5)

A World Heating Up

Global warming is already an indisputable reality as average world temperatures steadily rise. Last year being the hottest since recording began in 1860.

As the worlds weather hots up so there is an increase in the number and severity of storms, floods, landslides, hurricanes, tornadoes, droughts and fires. Pointing, as we shall observe in following chapters of this handbook, to calamitous conditions ahead.

Because of mankind's own folly: "The earth lies polluted under its inhabitants ...and its inhabitants suffer for their guilt." (Isa. 24: 5-6 New RSV)

Recognizing that global warming is a disaster largely attributable to the worlds own irresponsible behaviour, the Mirror newspaper warned in a recent arresting headline: "Our doomsday world is heading towards catastrophic boiling point unless global warming is halted."

Global warming much worse than predicted, say a body of the world's most distinguished meteorologists, members of the United Nation Inter-governmental Panel on climate change. These scientists report that the Earth is heating up much faster than expected pointing to consequences for human society likely to be catastrophic.

Christian Aid has warned of a nine-fold increase in climate-related disasters in the next twenty years, estimating that this will mean millions facing death from a spiral of catastrophes generated by global warming.

From the United Nations Environmental Programme has come a warning that devastation to property by global warming could bankrupt the world by 2065. Current disasters, the report says, would be dwarfed once global warming takes hold.

Satellite photographs show how global warming is now fracturing the polar ice caps and industrial pollution is choking the atmosphere.

Polar Melt Down Speeding Up

Average temperatures in Antarctica are reported to be rising at an alarming rate. Over the past ten years some two thousand square miles of its South Eastern tip have already melted.

Huge chunks of ice as much as 650ft thick and weighing up to fifty billion tons are breaking away and splitting into thousands of floating icebergs.

In the Arctic rising temperatures are also causing a significant melt. Sea ice has retreated by some ten to fifteen per cent since the 1950's and Arctic ice has, in some places, thinned by as much as forty per cent.

One of the most startling evidences of global warming in action today is the appearance of a mile wide patch of water at the North Pole, where the ice cap had previously been up to nine feet thick!

These melts are already beginning to cause a small rise in sea levels which, together with the expansion of sea waters as they become warmer, are set to lead to further significant rises.

Eventually large areas of low lying coastlands and islands in many parts of the world will be in real danger from encroaching seas: "on earth whole countries will be in despair afraid of the roar of the sea and the raging tides." (Luke 21.25)

Growth of Red Tide

Marine biologists are already researching a sea and fresh water condition known as Red Tide that is deadly towards fish, and is becoming more widespread as the world's seas begin to warm up.

It is known that Red Tide results from a growth spurt of single celled algae that turn the water reddish in colour when the temperature, salinity and nutrients in the water reach certain levels, prophesied ultimately to give whole areas of the sea the appearance of blood.

This is a judgement God has declared will come upon the world because it has: "poured out the blood of God's people and the prophets." (Rev. 16:6)

Greenhouse Gases Menace Goes On Increasing.

An unrelenting growth in world population each year, set to double over the next thirty years, brings with it a vast annual increase in the vaporous by-products of civilization so further adding to the continuous build up of dangerous "greenhouse gases" as one after another the developing countries add their increased emissions of these gases to the already vast discharges of the western nations.

Making matters worse is the continuing destruction by logging and fires of the CO_2 soaking up rain forests of the world.

Earth's Protective Ozone Layer - Under Growing Attack.

Enlarging holes in the earth's protective ozone layer are already allowing a significant increase in damaging ultra violet radiation, responsible for an alarming rate of increases in the number of cataracts and skin cancers and for weakening the human immune system making a variety of epidemics more difficult to control.

Scientists are warning that a plague of killer diseases will be unleashed and predict that there will be a dramatic return of malaria and the dreaded dengue fever to regions where they have been eradicated. The health impact it is warned will be on a scale not previously encountered by settled human society.

A sombre warning also comes from the World Health Organization that with the increase in temperature will come disasters "of almost Biblical proportions."

Massive epidemics caused by the spread of infections originating from "wild animals" (Rev. 6.8.). Already some 40 million people around the world are estimated to be HIV positive with the aids virus, a figure that is expected to rise to 100 million by 2005. A virus considered by many to have been transmitted to humans during medical research using body parts obtained from monkeys.

Scorching Middle East Temperatures.

In the hill country between the Dead Sea and the Red Sea lays a vast underground lake of pitch. As the searing heat of intensifying middle east global warming rises to a new and terrifying crescendo so this great pitch lake will begin to melt, and: "The rivers of Edom will turn into tar, and the soil will turn into sulphur." (Isa. 34.9.) Also beneath the land is methane gas, which released by an earthquake will cause the whole area suddenly to ignite, generating a violent explosion making: "such a noise that the entire earth will shake." (Jer. 49.21)

"Then the whole country will burn like tar. It will burn day and night, and smoke will rise from it for ever." (Isa. 34. 9-10)

At about this time also it seems: "The Lord will… bring a hot wind to dry up the Euphrates" (Isa. 11:15) and: "the water will be low in the Nile, and the river will gradually dry up. The channels of the river will stink as they slowly grow dry. Reeds and rushes will wither, and all the crops sown along the banks of the Nile will dry up and be blown away." (Isa. 19: 5-7)

As well as the rivers Euphrates and Nile: "The Lord will dry up the Gulf of Suez." (Isa. 11:15)

Of Egypt probably at about this time also God told Ezekiel: "I will set fire to Egypt" and "The land will be the most desolate in the world, and its cities will be left totally in ruins. When I set fire to Egypt" (Ezek. 30: 7-8 & 16).

When Climatic Changes Reach Their Peak

People the world over will suffer "Terrible and painful sores" (Rev. 16.2.) probably skin cancers and severe burns as: "the sun will be allowed to burn people with its fiery heat." (Rev. 16.8.) Stubborn to the end rather than turn to the Lord in repentance, people living at that time will curse "the God of heaven for their pains and sores. But they" will "not turn from their evil ways." (Rev. 16.11.)

As these climatic changes maximise: "huge hailstones, each weighing as much as fifty kilograms" will fall "from the sky on people" who will again curse God: "on account of the plague of hail because it" will be "such a terrible plague." (Rev. 16.21)

Hail is one of God's powerful weapons about which he says: "Have you ever visited the storerooms, where I keep the snow and the hail? I keep them ready for times of trouble, for days of battle and war." (Job 38.23)

God brought havoc upon the Egyptians with hail when they would not let the Israelites go: "The Lord sent a heavy hailstorm...It was the worst storm that Egypt had ever known in all its history. All over Egypt the hail struck down everything in the open, including all the people and all the animals. It beat down all the plants in the fields and broke all the trees. The region of Goshen, where the Israelites lived, was the only place where there was no hail (Exod. 9. 23-26).

Global warming a punishment brought about by breaking God's laws.

Global warming is a severe punishment allowed by God to come upon the nations of the world because they: "have defiled the earth by breaking God's laws and by violating the covenant he made to last for ever." (Isa. 24: 5)

A punishment already beginning with today's changing weather patterns, that will grow in intensity through the coming years and events described in the ensuing chapters of this handbook.

A Great Rescue Operation

Probably the first of the awesome world events predicted to follow God's "Red Alert" signal of 14th May 1948 will commence when the Lord Jesus: "will appear a second time, not to deal with sin, but to save those who are waiting for him." (Heb. 9.28) Those who have: "turned...to God, to serve the true and living God and to wait for his Son to come from heaven – his Son Jesus, whom he raised from death and who rescues us from God's anger that is coming." (1 Thess. 1. 9-10) For: "By his sacrificial death [Christian believers] are now put right with God; how much more, then, will we be saved by him from God's anger! (Rom. 5.9.)

The Great Rescue Operation.

This Divine rescue operation will be a massive lifting of all believing Christians up from the earth into heaven.

An operation described by Paul as a secret truth for Christians: "Listen to this secret truth" he says, "we shall not all die, but when the last trumpet sounds, we shall all be changed in an instant, as quickly as the blinking of an eye...For what is mortal must be changed into what is immortal; what will die must be changed into what cannot die. So when this takes place... Death is destroyed; victory is complete!" (1 Cor.15 51-54)

A vivid description of how this rescue will take place is also given by Paul: "The Lord himself will come down from heaven. Those who have died believing in Christ will rise to life first; then we who are living at that time will be gathered up along with them in the clouds to meet the Lord in the air. And so we will always be with the Lord. So then, encourage one another with these words." (1 Thess. 4. 16-18)

Until that time comes the apostle Paul urges all believing Christians: Set your hearts on the things that are in heaven…not on things here on earth" (Col.3.1-2) and "eagerly wait for our Saviour, the Lord Jesus Christ, to come from heaven" (Phil. 3.20). [See appendix]

Heavenly Exodus will Leave Chaos on Earth.

This vast and awesome removal of all believing Christians from earth to glory in heaven will clearly affect some countries to a much greater extent than others. Countries least affected will be nations with only a small number of Christians amongst their populations. Countries most affected will be those generally tolerant of and supportive of the Christian Faith.

Unavoidable casualties arising amongst those left behind on earth in the previously predominant Christian countries are bound to be widespread and dreadful. Aircraft, train, ship, coach, lorry and car crashes will be inevitable, as some of those in control are taken up to heaven.

Medical, fire-fighting and police services together with communication centres, power stations and water pumping stations will all come under emergency pressure, due to the sudden removal of Christians on their staffs.

Families will be divided. Christian believing parents and children being taken up to heaven while the non-believing members of their families are left behind.

Friends, neighbours and business colleagues will be separated. A feeling of utter loss and total desperation will come heavily upon many of those left behind as they recall how in the past they had heard, perhaps often, the gospel of Jesus, but for one reason or another failed to make a positive response: "They will perish because they did not welcome and love the truth so as to be saved." (2 Thess. 2:10) For then it will be impossible to escape the coming punishments, and: "The result is that all who have not believed the truth, but have taken pleasure in sin, will be condemned." (2 Thess. 2.12)

Confusion On Earth

The departure to heaven of so many people from all over the world will inevitably cause confusion on an immeasurable scale amongst registers of births, marriages and deaths, also in electoral lists, and in the records of licensing, taxation and health authorities.

The problem of identifying the missing gathered up ones will be greatly increased by the large number of fatalities attributable to the disasters on land, sea, and in the air during this vast human exodus.

Secret Arrival of Antichrist

In these unique conditions of mega chaos it is not hard to see how the mysterious man destined to become leader of the European Union might arrive on the earth virtually unnoticed.

He will appear: "at the proper time," when "the one who holds it (his appearing) back is taken out of the way." (2 Thess. 2.6-7) Then, he who "was once alive, but lives no longer" will "come up out of the abyss." (Rev. 17.8.)

However he travels from the abyss to earth, possibly by teleportation, this man will have arrived in the wake of probably the worlds greatest ever time of political confusion.

Known as: "The Wicked One" he "will come with the power of Satan and perform all kinds of false miracles and wonders, and use every kind of wicked deceit on those left behind. God sends the power of error to work in them so that they believe what is false." (2 Thess. 2. 9-11)

This man from the abyss will have a: "number (which) stands for a man's name." That "number is 666." (Rev. 13.18) To this man Satan will give: "his own power, his throne and his vast authority." (Rev. 13. 2.)

Resistance to Evil on the Earth Will Diminish

With the restraining influence of all true Christian believers gone from the earth, and with the arrival of his antichrist from the abyss, Satan's influence upon the world will be greatly exacerbated. Consequently he will seize his opportunity to extend the boundaries of his God-given authority as: "ruler of this world." (John 14.30)

A Face-Saving Deceit

Probably one of his first moves will be to energetically foster a face-saving deceit in an attempt to explain why so many known Bible believing Christians will have mysteriously disappeared.

This he may do by encouraging an occult teaching that is already being voiced in New Age circles. This teaching asserts that spiritual beings called "Higher Masters" will send their agents, the "Space Brothers", to remove from the earth all those whom they regard as narrow minded, bigoted Bible believers!

A removal they see as necessary to allow the Age of Aquarius to dawn. A time of spiritual unity. A time during which all the world religions will come together harmoniously, under the "Maitreya" to save the planet and mankind from destruction.

The Day Every Human Being will Tremble for Fear of God

The second of the awesome events predicted to come upon the world following God's "Red Alert" signal of May 1948 will be a Russian led Moslem invasion of Israel. On that day the Middle East will explode! For: "the Sovereign Lord says... I will be furious. I declare in the heat of my anger that on that day...every...human being on the face of the earth will tremble for fear of me." (Ezek. 38. 18-20)

At this time God will say to Russia: "I will send you to invade my land in order to show the nations who I am, to show my holiness by what I do through you. You are the one I was talking about long ago, when I announced through my servants, the prophets of Israel, that in days to come I would bring someone to attack Israel. The Sovereign Lord has spoken." (Ezek. 38. 16-17)

The illustration given to Ezekiel by God in announcing that Russia will be drawn to attack Israel is powerful indeed. In the time of Ezekiel when prisoners of war were taken to be made slaves they were sometimes controlled by a chain fastened to a sharply pointed hook that had been thrust through the prisoner's lower jaw. Any resistance on the part of the captive to a directional tug was so painful that an obedient response was fast and certain. When God said to Ezekiel of Russia: "I will turn him round, put hooks in his jaws, and drag him and all his troops away," (Ezek. 38.4.) he was emphasising that Russia would be in no position to resist that pressure.

In his book "The Last Dash South" Vladimir Zhirinovsky, a flamboyant member of the Russian Parliament writes, "there is only one option. We must carry out this operation code named "The Last Dash South"…this is not just my whim. It is Russia's destiny. It is fate."

Such a move might be viewed by Russia's generals as an ideal operation to secure a speedy and popular victory that would regain the lost prestige of it's tattered forces, and at the same time please it's own often turbulent and troublesome southern Islamic states.

Israel's Mistaken Feeling of Safety.

There is a time coming when Israel - probably through the signing of a peace settlement with the Palestinian authority or by reason of maintaining a military stranglehold on their militant terrorists – believe that they: "Live in safety." (Ezek. 38.8)

This will not be the way it will look to Israel's enemies who will see her as: "a helpless country where the people live in peace and security in unwalled towns that have no defences." (Ezek. 38.11)

Arab Nation Committed to Destroy Israel

Many centuries ago Israel's Arab neighbours declared: "let us destroy their nation, so that Israel will be forgotten for ever…we will take for our own the land that belongs to God." (Psalm 83. 4 & 12) A threat repeated many times since.

In the 1960's Egypt's ruler Gamal Nasser reaffirmed on behalf of the Arab nations: "our basic objective will be the destruction of Israel."

Only recently Arafat has said: "We have a date to raise the Palestinian flag over Jerusalem's walls, minarets and churches. They say it is far fetched but we know it is near and we are right. We will stand and work together until we raise the Palestinian flag over Jerusalem."

Together Moslem nations occupy a gigantic, hostile surrounding land mass, many times the size of Israel. Possessing immense wealth gained from oil revenues. The size of their populations and military forces exceed many times those of Israel.

Palestine Never An Arab State

In spite of the Palestinian claim history reveals that there has never been an independent, politically established state of Palestine!

Although the population living in the land has been principally Arab, they have always been under the rule of an occupying state or mandatory power.

Over the years, since 1948, Russia has developed considerable military links with the Middle East Moslem nations. Particularly with those countries named by Ezekiel as fellow invaders of Israel: "Tell him [Russia] to get ready and have all his troops ready at his command." (Ezek. 38.7.) "Men from Persia [Iran], Sudan and Libya are with him [Russia], and all have shields and helmets. All the fighting men of the lands of Gomer and Beth Togarmah in the north are with him, and so are men from many other nations." (Ezek. 38.5-6)

Identification of the modern day people of Gomer is not certain and several possibilities exist as to their whereabouts. It seems likely, however, that many of them may be citizens of the Russian commonwealth nations.

The people of Beth Togermah are likely to be found today living in the southern Islamic Russian countries, Turkey, and probably northern Iraq.

There will also be: "Men from many other nations" (Ezek. 38.6.) enlisting in this great invasion force. Armies likely to be included will almost certainly be from other Middle-Eastern Moslem nations.

Iraq is another significant enemy of Israel, and is currently believed to be busily engaged in the development of mass-destruction ballistic missiles. Reportedly much of the work being done in Libya and Sudan.

Most powerful of all Middle east countries after Israel is Egypt with a large well equipped airforce, a highly mechanized army and a sizeable navy with many small, fast missile-firing craft.

Invasion Begins with Massive Air Armada

A large military force from Russia in: "the far north" (Ezek. 38.15) will suddenly swoop southwards down towards Israel and: "will attack like a storm and cover the land like a cloud" (Ezek. 38.9).

Truly a remarkable prophetic portrayal of how a today's aerial bombardment with its flashes across the sky and thunderous sounds echoing around would be.

Attacking armies, will also it seems move on Israel from Iran, Sudan, Libya and other surrounding nations.

Probably Russia will claim her invasion to be a "Nato style" operation to save the Palestinian people from alleged Israeli oppression.

On arrival in the land of Israel however things will turn out to be very different, as the invading troops out of control run amok. Ravaging factories, shops and homes: "You will plunder and loot the people who live in cities." (Ezek. 38.12) Prompting the watching world, much of it probably still in chaos from the great gathering-up into heaven of believing Christians, to make a diplomatic protest: "Have you assembled your army and attacked in order to loot and plunder? Do you intend to get silver and gold, livestock and property, and to march off with all those spoils?" (Ezek. 38.13)

Invading Forces Terrified by Giant Earthquake

The attackers will very soon find themselves in a desperate situation. For: "on that day there will be a severe earthquake in the land of Israel. Every fish and bird, every animal large and small, and every human being on the face of the earth will tremble for fear of me. Mountains will fall, cliffs will crumble and every wall will collapse. I will terrify Gog [Russian leader] with all sorts of calamities. I, the Sovereign Lord, have spoken". (Ezek. 38. 19-21)

Such a devastating earthquake with its epicentre in Israel will be bound to cause chaos in the command structure of the large cosmopolitan invading forces with their widely differing cultures, languages and shades of skin.

Ezekiel makes no mention of any battle engagements between the invading armies and Israel's powerful defence forces. Probably both sides at that time will be entirely taken up with extracting themselves from the earthquakes devastation.

It seems that Israel's mighty "Second Strike" nuclear deterrent, with a believed capacity to destroy simultaneously the capital cities of the invaders, may not be fired.

In all the turmoil, chaos, confusion and panic generated by this massive world-shaking earthquake, the distraught, bewildered and frightened foreign troops will flee to the mountains for cover.

Invaders Weapons of Mass Destruction Misfire Upon Themselves.

Upon this motley rabble of uncontrollable and terrified men, God will unleash "all sorts of calamities."

They will: "turn their swords against one another," (Ezek. 38.21) killing thousands.

Centuries earlier when the people of Israel were in similar danger God had saved them in the very same way: "The Lord threw the invading armies into a panic. The Ammonites and the Moabites attacked the Edomite army and completely destroyed it, and then they turned on each other in savage fighting. When the Judean army reached a tower that was in the desert, they looked towards the enemy and saw that they were all lying on the ground dead. Not one had escaped." (2 Chron. 20: 22-24)

Part of an initial attack by Syria might be a barrage of scud missiles. Some of which might be carrying chemical warheads.

How God will bring about confusion, chaos and destruction amongst these invading forces is not clear. One interesting possibility however is by a solar flare causing electrical disruptions to radio transmissions and navigational systems. Opening up the possibility of the aggressors being destroyed by their own sophisticated deadly weapons as they wrestle in vain with blackouts and distortions affecting targeting and firing systems. Alternatively some of Iraq's unmanned drone planes equipped to deliver chemical or biological weapons might be blown off course and spray the invading armies with their own deadly poisons for: "He [God] sends the wind in front of him…it sweeps nations to destruction and puts an end to their evil plans." (Isa. 30. 28)Which ever way it happens it seems the diabolical "swords" of the invaders may well prove to be the very weapons of destruction which the Lord will use to kill thousands of them. For many will die of terrible diseases: "I will punish them with disease." (Ezek. 38.22)

Aggressors flee as God Rains Down His Own Powerful Weapons.

Then, upon these distraught and dejected invaders: "Torrents of rain and hail, together with fire and sulphur will pour down on him and his army and on the many nations that are on his side." (Ezek. 38.22.).

All the sophistication and power of man's modern weaponry will be but fragile toys against such rushing water, pounding hail, and against the fire and sulphur flowing down from the volcanic eruptions high above them.

So it will be that uncountable thousands of the invaders will be destroyed as they flee from God's anger.

God's armoury is full of weapons against which mere man has no defence: "More powerful than all armies is he." (Psalm 47.9.) For, says God: "Have you ever visited the storerooms, where I keep the snow and the hail? I keep them ready for times of trouble, for days of battle and war...Can you shout orders to the clouds and make them drench you with rain? And, if you command the lightning to flash, will it come to you and say: 'At your service?'" (Job. 38. 22-23 & 34-36)

To the prophet Jeremiah it was revealed about God: "he brings clouds from the ends of the earth. He makes lightening flash in the rain and sends the winds from his storeroom. At the sight of this, men feel stupid and senseless." (Jer. 51. 16-17)

Way back in Joshua's time: "While the Amorites were running down the pass from the Israelite army, the Lord made large hailstones fall down on them all the way to Azekah. More were killed by the hailstones than by the Israelites. (Josh. 10.11-12)

For hail is one of God's powerful weapons stored ready for: "days of battle and war." (Job 38.23)

After the rain and hail: "Fire and sulphur will pour down on him and his army and on the many nations that are on his side." (Ezek. 38.22.)

This God-given revelation to Ezekiel of the coming invasion of Israel makes it abundantly clear that the massive attack will be frustrated and the invading armies crushed by the immeasurably powerful and irresistible hand of God.

Thousands upon thousands of dead soldiers will lie strewn among the fallen mountains, crumbled cliffs, volcanic cinders and floodwater sludge, and in the debris of broke-down trees and buildings: "Gog [the Russian leader] and his army and his allies will fall dead on the mountains of Israel and I will let their bodies be food for all the birds and wild animals." (Ezek. 39.4.)

Clearing Up Operations Begin

Although Israeli losses are not specifically stated, it does seem likely that they will receive a substantial measure of Divine protection. For during the next seven months they will, no doubt using heavy earth moving machinery, collect vast numbers of dead invaders bodies from the mountain area and bury them in a giant new cemetery in "Travellers Valley", a vale to the east of the

Dead Sea which will from then on be called: "The Valley of Gog's Army."

It will take the Israelites seven months to bury all the corpses and make the land clean again." (Ezek. 39.11-12.) Everyone in the land of Israel will be conscripted to help in this grisly task. Abandoned battlefield equipment will also be gathered up for burning.

Invaders Homelands to be Attacked with Fire.

Using the powerful weapons of his creation, the Lord Almighty will not only destroy the invading armies on the mountains of Israel, but he will then attack their homelands: "I will start a fire in the land of Magog [Russia] and along all the coasts where people live undisturbed and everyone will know that I am the Lord." (Ezek. 39.6.)

Ezekiel reveals no details of how these widespread fires will be started, or of their full extent.

Upon these homelands of: "the many nations that are on his [the Russian leaders] side" the Lord will also: "pour down the same terrors" that he used to destroy their combatant armies in Israel: "Torrents of rain, and hail, together with fire and sulphur" (Ezek. 38.22).

This devastating judgement upon Russia and the Islamic invaders nations will be God's punishment against them for their Christ rejection and Godlessness, as well as for their savage attack on Israel.

In meting out this punishment the extent to which God will use intensifying global warming to bring about his punishments is not clear: "in this way" God says: "I will show all the nations that I am great and that I am holy. They will know then that I am the Lord." (Ezek. 38: 23) Israel too: "will know from then on that I am the Lord their God." (Ezek. 39:22)

In the Wake of the Battle

Into the fire ravaged countries of the armies that had attacked them the Israeli forces will now enter and: "they will loot and plunder those who looted and plundered them." (Ezek. 39.10) Remaining amongst the rest of the world there will be a real fear of God's anger should they oppose Israel. For by: "Then the nations will know that I, the Lord, am the Holy God of Israel" (Ezek. 39.7.).

After they are finally extinguished, the great fires over the invaders lands will have left in their path huge-scale loss of life, destruction and famine requiring relief and rebuilding on an unprecedented scale.

Probably at this time Israel's Borders Expanded.

It will probably be at this time that Israel will extend her borders to take in the whole of the land God promised to Jacob: "I am the Lord, the God of Abraham and Isaac," he said, "I will give to you and your descendants this land on which you are lying... they will extend their territory in all directions and through you and your descendants I will bless all the nations." (Gen. 28. 13-14)

To Abraham God had already said: "I promise to give to your descendants all the land from the border of Egypt to the River Euphrates." (Gen. 15.18.)

To achieve this extension of their boundaries the Israelis must annex parts at least of present day Syria, Lebanon, Jordan, Iraq and Saudi Arabia.

With these countries still reeling from God's judgement of fire, Israel's forces are likely to swiftly complete their operations which will then provide Israel with a land area in total something similar to that of France today.

A New Temple in Jerusalem

In Israel at that time there will be a return to Temple worship that will be made possible by the speedy building of a new Temple on the site previously occupied by the Islamic Dome of the Rock Mosque. For this mosque it seems almost certainly will have been destroyed by the world-shaking earthquake with which God will have opened his onslaught on the invading Russian and Islamic armies: "every wall will collapse" (Ezek. 38.20). In this new Temple the Israelis will recommence the "sacrifices and offerings" (Dan. 9.27) of Temple worship, and will return to the priesthood.

European Union and Peace Treaty

Even the immensely strong European Union will be amazed at God's utter destruction of Israel's invaders and their homelands, and will seek co-operation rather than confrontation. This they will do by commencing negotiations for a seven years peace agreement with Israel.

Power Balance Shifted

The balance of European and Middle Eastern power at this time will undergo radical changes, for after God metes out his devastating punishments upon Russia and her Islamic allies they will retain little or no world influence.

On the other hand, the vast European Union will have been gradually coming together and growing in strength. A process that began with the "Benelux" alliance between Belgium, Holland and Luxembourg in 1948, and later expanded with the treaty of Rome in 1957, first in to the European Common market, and now, in its much enlarged and developed form, into the European Union. Committed to work towards full political, economic, financial and military unity.

Also in 1948 Britain, France and the "Benelux" countries came together in a mutual defence alliance that became known as The Western European Union. Later they were joined by Germany, Greece, Italy, Portugal and Spain.

These ten western European nations were all previously part of the Old Roman Empire and began the military revival predicted to grow into: "A fourth empire that will be on the earth and will be different from all other empires. It will crush the whole earth and trample it down" (Dan. 7.23). This under its Satan empowered leader from the abyss.

This ten nations European military organisation then joined up with the USA to form the North Atlantic Treaty Organisation (NATO), and set up the military arm of The European Union.

Membership of the European Union.

The introduction of a single European currency for trading by credit card, cheque or other form of money transfer has been in operation for some time, although at present not all members of the Union have joined the system. The Euro is now quoted daily on the world's money markets, is increasingly being used in world trade and from this current year onwards has become common currency in the Union.

The European Union currently comprises Austria, Belgium, Britain, Denmark, Finland, France, Germany, Greece, Holland, Ireland, Italy, Luxembourg, Portugal, Spain, and Sweden.

Applications for membership are in hand from Bulgaria, Cyprus, The Czech Republic, Estonia, Hungary, Latvia, Lithuania, Malta, Poland, Romania, Slovakia, Switzerland and Turkey.

Further applications will no doubt follow and all the time the Union's world influence and power continues to grow.

Currently a European Commission President with twenty Commissioners, and an elected European Parliament of 626 members supported by some 30,000 employed staff working in 11 different languages provide the political government of the Union.

Ten Man Ruling Cabinet and the Anti-christ.

The next step in the Union's government it seems from scripture will be the appointment of a ten man ruling cabinet that will assume overall control of political, fiscal, economic and military affairs.

Then an eleventh and mysterious leader will join these ten who will: "all have the same purpose" which will be to "give their power and authority to the beast" (Rev. 17.13), scriptures name for the mysterious new European Leader who will earlier have secretly appeared from the abyss.

The Unions problems at this time will be great. It will remain: "a divided empire...part of the empire will be strong and part of it weak." (Dan. 2. 41-42) Its: "people will be a mixture and will not remain united." (Dan. 2. 43. NIV)

The ten European leaders, over burdened with the problems of the time, and having recognized this man's immense intelligence, dynamic energy and exceptional political insight will then unanimously appoint him their leader.

All this was shown to the prophet Daniel: " ten kings...will rule this empire. Then another king will appear, he will be very different from the earlier ones and will overthrow three kings." (Dan. 7.24.)

This man will become leader through the power of Satan that will have been given him.

In this connection it is worth noting that Satan's: "throne" (Rev. 2.13.) was transferred from Pergamon in the late 1800's to Germany, and re-erected in Berlin by Kaiser Wilhelm II in 1902. This massive 'Altar', now central to the Pergamon Museum in Berlin, was where the martyrdom of early Christians frequently took place. In 1934 Hitler commissioned an exact copy to be made for his Nazi rallies in Nuremberg. Here, from 'Satan's Seat', he decreed death to the Jews. Perhaps this may become the chosen seat of authority for the man from the abyss.

Soon after being given his office, this man will remove three of the ten leaders. Then by exerting his strong personality over the remaining seven will elevate himself to the position of Dictator in the vast European Union.

Recently the EU built a new 8 billion pound Parliament Building in Strasbourg having a remarkable resemblance to Pieter Breughel's famous painting the Tower of Babel. A tower built to defy God: "Now let's build…a Tower that reaches the sky, so that we can make a name for ourselves." (Gen. 11.4.)

The False Prophet and World Church

About this time will emerge a prominent and influential personage. A man who will establish himself as a kind of primate of all faiths and be actively engaged in cementing together in one ecumenical world church all the religious activities and ceremonies then taking place around the world.

Probably building upon the foundation already laid down by the currently expanding United Religions Organization. A body with its roots in the World Council of Churches that began in 1948 in Amsterdam as a Council of Christian churches but which in 1970 widened its aims to be a World Council embracing all faiths, with its headquarters in Geneva.

Many years ago God warned that he will not tolerate being associated with other god's: "After the Philistines captured the Covenant Box, they…took it into the temple of their god Dagon and set it up beside his statue. Early next morning the people of Ashdod saw that the statue of Dagon had fallen face downwards on the ground in front of the Lord's Covenant Box. So they lifted it up and put it back in its place. Early the following morning they saw that the statue had again fallen down in front of the Covenant Box. This time its head and both its arms were broken off and were lying in the doorway…The Lord punished the people of Ashdod severely and terrified them" (1 Sam. 5. 1-6).

The False Prophet will be gentle, like a lamb, but his doctrine and practices will be fierce like a dragon. A vision of this man was given to John on Patmos and revealed to him as a beast that: "had two horns like a lambs horns, and spoke like a dragon." (Rev.

13.11.) He will deceive the people of all nations by his power to perform miracles.

John saw in another vision that this religious potentate "performed great miracles...made fire come out of heaven to earth in the sight of everyone and...deceived all people living on earth by means of the miracles which it was allowed to perform in the presence of the first beast." (Rev. 13. 13-14)

No doubt this deceiver will remind those who witness this display that centuries earlier it was by fire from heaven that Elijah's credentials were confirmed by God! "Elijah approached the altar and prayed 'O Lord, the God of Abraham, Isaac and Jacob, prove now that...I am your servant...' the Lord sent fire down, and it burnt the sacrifice, the wood, and the stones, scorched the earth and dried up the water in the trench. When the people saw this, they threw themselves on the ground and exclaimed, 'the Lord is God, the Lord alone is God'" (1 Kings 18. 36-39)

144,000 Jewish Preachers

With God's awesome destruction of Israel's invaders still fresh in the minds of people everywhere, and global warming increasing in intensity God will appoint 144,000 Jewish Evangelists, 12,000 from each tribe, to go out over the whole world and seek to turn men and women and boys and girls to himself.

These: "servants of our God", [angels] will mark "with a seal on their foreheads" (Rev. 7.3.) and they will be preserved by God to minister his Gospel of Salvation, in opposition to the False Prophet, world religious leader until the end of the age.

The message proclaimed by these Evangelists seems likely to be similar to that preached by John the Baptist: "Turn away from your sins...because the Kingdom of Heaven is near!" (Matt. 3.2.) Looking back towards the cross in contrast to John the Baptist's looking forward to it, these Evangelists will surely preach of the Lord Jesus Christ and his sacrifice as: "The Lamb of God, who takes away the sin of the world!" (John 1.29)

The Tyrannical Dictator Breaks His Pledge

Halfway through the seven year peace treaty that the European Dictator will have signed with Israel, he will break it, and will be: "allowed to fight against God's people and to defeat them" (Rev. 13.7.). Then "God's people will be under his power for three and a half years". (Dan. 7.25)

During these three and a half years this audacious man will perpetuate a catalogue of blasphemies against God, and vicious atrocities against the Jewish people: "The beast was allowed to make proud claims which were insulting to God and it [he] was permitted to have authority for forty two months. It [he] began to curse God, his name, and the place where he lives, and all those who live in heaven." (Rev. 13. 5-6)

Claiming to be God in His Temple

Before long he will: "put an end to [Jewish] sacrifices and offerings" (Dan 9.27) and as the ultimate blasphemy and challenge to God: "will even go in and sit down in God's Temple and claim to be God." (2 Thess. 2.4.)

To strengthen his claim to be a god he will order an image of himself to be set up in the Temple by the Religious leader. This image to be an object of worship into which the Religious leader will be allowed to breathe life [not human life]: "so that the image could talk and put to death all those who would not worship it" (Rev. 13.15).

Listening and speaking computers are already in use. These computers can audibly recognize and verbally reply to a wide range of questions when put to them.

With such incredible surges forward in technical achievements it is no longer difficult to foresee a virtual reality image of the Tyrannical World Dictator in the Temple being able to interrogate, and pronounce judgement on those brought before it. Automatically putting to death all whose answers are not the required ones.

At this time the European Union Dictator will demand undivided worship of himself and his image in the Temple. To get this he will dismiss the Religious Primate from office and disband the World church.

Time to Escape from Judaea

Jesus warns those who will be living in Judaea at that most dreadful of all times to: "run away to the hills" as soon as they recognize the sign of the image in the Temple: "A man who is on the roof of his house must not take the time to go down and get his belongings from his house. A man who is in the field must not go back to get his cloak. How terrible it will be in those days for women who are pregnant and for mothers with little babies!" (Matt. 24. 15-22)

For those in Judaea who speedily run away to the hills, there will be awaiting them on arrival a place of safety where they: "will be taken care of for 1,260 days" (Rev. 12.6.).

Seemingly placing this event at the time when the European Union Dictator will break his 7 year peace agreement with Israel when only half of its time has run.

Scripture does not say how God will provide for these Judaeans but it may be in the same way that he did so once before when their ancestors escaped from slavery in Egypt. Then they were promised in the desert: "it is the Lord who will give you meat to eat in the evening [quails] and as much bread as you want in the morning" [made from manna] (Exo. 16.8.) detailed description that appeared on the ground every morning except on the Sabbath.

Satan Thrown Down to Earth

It will probably be about this time that : "war broke out in heaven. Michael and his angels fought against the dragon, [Satan] who fought back with his angels; but the dragon was defeated, and he and his angels were not allowed to stay in heaven any longer. The huge dragon was thrown out – that ancient serpent, called the Devil, or Satan, that deceived the whole world. He was thrown down to earth, and all his angels with him...how terrible for the earth and the sea! For the Devil has come down to you, and he is filled with rage, because he knows that he has only a little time left." (Rev. 12: 7-12)

God's Two Witnesses

Also at about this time God will send into Jerusalem his two special witnesses. Their mission to proclaim God's message for that terrible time: "I will send my two witnesses dressed in sackcloth, and they will proclaim God's message during those 1,260 days." (Rev. 11.3.)

These two witnesses will, for the time of their ministry, enjoy Divine protection: "If anyone tries to harm them, fire comes out of their mouths and destroys their enemies; and in this way, whoever tries to harm them will be killed" (Rev. 11.5.).

Back in Old Testament history, King Ahaziah sent an officer with fifty men to arrest the prophet Elijah, but: "fire came down and killed the officer and his men. The king sent another officer with fifty men" the same thing happened to them "At once the fire of God came down and killed the officer and his men." The king sent a third officer with another fifty men, but he had heard of the fate of his two fellow officers and their troops and so "fell on his knees in front of Elijah, and pleaded, 'Man of God, be merciful to me and my men. Spare our lives!' (2 Kings 1. 10-13)

These two witnesses will also: "have authority to shut up the sky so that there will be no rain during the time they proclaim

God's message" (Rev. 11.6.). The same authority that had been given to the prophet Elijah back in Old Testament days when Ahab was king of Israel. Because of great sin in Israel, Elijah told the king: "'In the name of the Lord, the living God of Israel, whom I serve, I tell you that there will be no dew or rain for the next two or three years until I say so'...after some time, in the third year of the drought, the Lord said to Elijah, 'Go and present yourself to King Ahab, and I will send rain'...In a little while the sky was covered with dark clouds, the wind began to blow, and heavy rain began to fall'" (1 Kings. 16.30; 17.1; 18.1; & 45).

Furthermore, the two witnesses will: "have authority also over the springs of water, to turn them into blood," and will "have authority also to strike the earth with every kind of plague as often as they wish" (Rev. 11.6.).

During the time of Israel's slavery in Egypt: "Aaron raised his stick and struck the surface of the river, and all the water in it was turned to blood. The fish in the river died, and it smelt so bad that the Egyptians could not drink from it" (Exod. 7. 20-21).

Thus it is that God has already demonstrated in Old Testament history virtually the whole range of powers that will be given to his two witnesses at this time.

The powerful preaching of the 144,000 Jewish Evangelists will lead thousands to repent and turn to the Lord. Refusing to receive the mark, that would signify their acceptance of the World Dictator as a god.

Then: "When they [the two witnesses] finish proclaiming their message, the beast [European Dictator by now World Dictator] that comes up out of the abyss will fight against them. He will defeat them and kill them, and their bodies will lie in the street of the great city, where their Lord was crucified...People from all nations, tribes, languages and races will look at their bodies for three and a half days and will not allow them to be buried" (Rev. 11. 7-9).

It seems that the World Dictator and Religious Leader will then declare a world-wide public holiday to celebrate this apparent victory over God's two witnesses. On that day: "The people of the earth will be happy because of the death of these two. They will celebrate and send presents to each other, because those two prophets brought much suffering upon mankind" (Rev. 11.10).

Probably these celebrations will include a television report from Jerusalem, confirming the death of God's two witnesses by transmitting pictures of them lying dead in the street.

Resurrection of God's Two Witnesses.

Then, suddenly the cameras will catch a movement! For: "after three and a half days a life-giving breath came from God and entered them, and they stood up; and all who saw them were terrified. Then, the two prophets heard a loud voice say to them from heaven, 'Come up here!' As their enemies watched, they went up into heaven in a cloud. At that moment there was a violent earthquake; a tenth of the city was destroyed, and seven thousand people were killed. The rest of the people were terrified, and praised the greatness of the God in heaven" (Rev. 11. 11-13).

This return to worship of: "the God in heaven" it seems will be only short lived for about this time it appears an assassination attempt will be made upon the World Dictator who will be: "wounded by the sword" (Rev. 13.14.). He: "seemed to have been fatally wounded, but the wound had healed. The whole earth was amazed and followed the beast" (Rev. 13.3.). Indeed his survival will so impress the world that: "All people living on earth will worship it [him], except those whose names were written before the creation of the world in the book of the living which belongs to [Jesus] the Lamb that was killed" (Rev. 13.8.).

Anti-Christ World Dictator

Having defeated and occupied Israel by force the World Dictator will be given by Satan: "authority over every tribe, nation, language and race" (Rev. 13.7.), and will confirm himself not only as World Dictator but as a god!

It is probable that much of his power over the nations will be gained by political, economic and fiscal manoeuvres. Some countries however will only be brought under his control by military might and to this end: "he will invade many countries, like the water of a flood" (Dan. 11.40).

In Israel there will be severe famine due to the drastic global warming, supervolcano eruption, two asteroid strikes and a violent earthquake. On top of these natural disasters will come the added judgements brought by God's two witnesses.

Regulations will be introduced and to be able to draw rations it will be necessary to have a mark, probably a small microchip implant, either on the right hand or on the forehead. A mark that will only be granted to those who will turn to worshipping the World Dictator or his image. No one will be allowed to: "buy or sell unless he has this mark" (Rev. 13. 16-17).

Many thousands will be martyred because of refusing this mark, scripture says: "never again will they hunger [they had suffered starvation] or thirst [the water had been polluted]; neither sun nor any scorching heat will burn them" [they had suffered the sun burning of acute global warming] (Rev. 7.16).

Terrible and Painful Sores

At this time: "Terrible and painful sores appeared on those who had the mark of the beast and on those who had worshipped its image" (Rev. 16.2.). Prophecy reveals that: "Darkness fell over the beast's kingdom, and people bit their tongues because of their pain, and they cursed the God of heaven for their pains and sores. But they did not turn from their evil ways." (Rev. 16.10-11).

Also at this time: "They were burnt by the fierce heat, and they cursed the name of God, who has authority over these plagues. But they would not turn from their sins and praise his greatness." (Rev. 16.9.) Then: "Huge hailstones, each weighing as much as fifty kilogrammes, fell from the sky on people, who cursed God on account of the plague of hail, because it was such a terrible plague." (Rev. 16.21.)

Of this time Jesus prophesied: "the trouble at that time will be far more terrible than any there has ever been, from the beginning of the world...nor will there ever be anything like it again. But God has already reduced the number of days; had he not done so, nobody would survive." (Matt. 24.21-22.).

Four other major Divine punishments also take place during the three and a half years after the World Dictator breaks his pledge with Israel. In order to better describe these they are dealt with in two separate chapters that follow, headed: "Supervolcano Eruption" and "Coming Asteroid Strikes", and "Alien Invaders Land on Earth."

The final judgement disaster of this three and a half years of great tribulation will be reached when all the nations of the world are drawn together by the power of Satan for the battle of Armageddon. The most dreadful and destructive of all earthly battles that is the subject of a later chapter in this handbook headed: "Armageddon Ends Man's Rule on Earth".

Supervolcano Eruption and Asteroid Strikes

Through a vision given to John on the Island of Patmos God revealed three catastrophic natural disasters destined to come upon the earth. Probably, just after the European Union Dictator reneges on his peace treaty with Israel and occupies Jerusalem.

The first of these three Divine judgements, known in scripture as "The Trumpet Judgements", is one of the most awesome of all the apocalyptic events. Predicted to devastate by fire no less than one third of the entire earth's surface!

One Third of the Earth on Fire

In his vision John saw: "Hail and fire, mixed with blood, came pouring down on the earth. A third of the earth was burnt up, a third of the trees, and every blade of green grass" (Rev. 8.7.). Inevitably, with such widespread fires, loss of life over a third of the earth will be on a horrendous scale such as never known before. Damage to food crops, public services, buildings and infrastructures will understandably be on a massive scale.

Supervolcano Eruption

Modern science is continually confirming the plausibility of a growing number of biblical, End of the Age predictions. Some of which have hitherto seemed unexplainable.

Because scripture provides no information on the generating force behind this predicted mega disaster it is to science we turn for a possible solution. This brings into the frame of plausibility a supervolcano eruption.

Of supervolcanoes Professor Bill McGuire, University College, London says, "these things…are absolutely apocalyptic in scale." Professor Michael Rampino, New York University says, "We can't really overstate the effect of these huge eruptions. Civilisation will start to creak at the seams." And Professor Robert Smith, University of Utah says, "it would be extremely devastating on a scale that we've probably never even thought about."

Yellowstone National Park

A widely publicised BBC TV programme in the Horizon series recently gave a spine chilling insight into the destruction a supervolcano such as the one in Yellowstone National Park, USA might cause if it were to erupt.

Volcanologists predict such an eruption would cause total extinction of life in the most vulnerable areas with severe damage to the whole of a North American continent.

There would then be a short delay before resulting massive global climate changes produced by dense dust clouds from the eruption, blocking out the suns light and heat, would for probably up to a year, reduce all human life on the planet to near starvation.

Supervolcanoes are many times more lethal than even the most powerful of ordinary volcanoes. They are not, like ordinary volcanoes, mountains with craters at their summits, but depressions in the ground. Beneath which depressions lie huge collapsed craters called Calderas.

In a supervolcano eruption vast quantities of molten rock, ash and dust would be hurled high into the atmosphere, along with clouds of sulphur dioxide and other gases, which would eventually come pouring down upon the earth burning up everything on which if fell.

Geologists say that in the case of Yellowstone Park an eruption is now overdue. Ground surface bulging, and other signs measured by satellite suggest this vast supervolcano, which measures approximately 70 x 30 km, is on the move.

Another, but perhaps less likely, source of this first "Trumpet Judgement" might be an incoming asteroid which fragments on entering the earth's atmosphere, showering a third of the earth with burning rocks.

Asteroids Strike the Earth

The second and third "Trumpet Judgements" predicted to follow are two asteroid strikes one upon the earth and the other into the sea. Further Divine judgements upon a world who: "reject God and who do not obey the Good News about our Lord Jesus" (2 Thess. 1.8.).

Scripture paints an awesome prophetic picture in which something that looked like a: "huge mountain on fire was thrown into the sea. A third of the sea was turned into blood, a third of the living creatures in the sea died, and a third of the ships were destroyed" (Rev. 8. 8-9).

The vast tidal wave bound to ensue as a result of this massive splash down will mean: "On earth whole countries will be in despair, afraid of the roar of the sea and the raging tides (Luke 21.25).

Something like a "huge mountain on fire" is a remarkably accurate picture of how a giant asteroid might look as it enters the earth's atmosphere, generating immense heat in the process.

Scripture next reveals how John was shown a second prophetic picture that revealed how: "A large star, burning like a torch, dropped from the sky and fell on a third of the rivers and on the springs of water. A third of the water turned bitter, and many people died from drinking the water, because it had turned bitter" (Rev. 8. 10-11).

It seems from this account that the second giant asteroid will on impact send up into the atmosphere clouds of toxic particles which will fall into a third of the Earth's rivers, lakes and reservoirs making them acid, bitter and poisonous to drink.

Twilight Over the Earth

As a result of the combined volume of debris, ash and dust sent high into the atmosphere from these three mighty judgements: "A third of the sun was struck, and a third of the moon, and a third of the stars, so that their light lost a third of its brightness" (Rev. 8.12).

Such a significant reduction in the world's light and heat will add considerably to the already drastic climate changes then being suffered on account of acute global warming.

Asteroids on the Loose

A recent headline in The Express newspaper reports that astronomers are warning of a catastrophic future for mankind on the grounds that there are some 200 asteroids "on the loose in our part of the solar system," and that "many may be on orbits which could one day put them on a collision course with the earth."

Dr. Duncan Steel, of The University of Salford it was reported, told the UK National Astronomy Meeting in Cambridge recently that one asteroid which seems to have gone missing is cause for particular concern.

It was last seen for ten days in 1998, and looked then as if it might be on a potential collision course with the Earth, probably within the next 30 years. The rock is about half a mile across and would obliterate most of the British Isles if they were struck by it. The chances of that occurring are small, but the consequences so phenomenal that it is a hazard we must take seriously, said Dr. Steel.

In an edition of The Independent on Sunday a headline announced, "End of the world is (almost) nigh." Below this headline the feature went on to say, "It's official: the Earth is at risk from falling asteroids crashing to Earth."

"Apocalypse postponed" announced a recent *Daily Mail* headline. This feature went on, "it appeared without warning, a massive chunk of rock hurtling towards us at 20 miles a second."

The article continued that although the asteroid missed the Earth it did so only by "an astro-whisker" just some 130,000 miles beyond our moon. A distance reckoned by astronomers to be too close for comfort.

The rock, code named 2001 YB5 had it struck London everything within 100 miles would have been devastated with severe damage occurring for a further 500 miles.

Had the asteroid landed in the sea it would have caused a tidal wave large enough to submerge much of Britain. YB5 is on a 1321 day elliptical orbit of the sun.

Asteroid Tracking System Set Up

NASA has set up a task force called The Near-earth Asteroid Tracking System. Designed to collect sufficient information about possible asteroid threats to enable them to prepare preventative action should one be found on a course likely to bring it into contact with the earth. This was the tracking system that discovered the asteroid 2001 YB5.

NASA's spacecraft known as 'Near Probe' is already orbiting an asteroid so closely that one of its solar panels brushed against the surface of the asteroid.

Attempts will certainly be made to divert the threat of any imminent asteroid strike upon the earth, the concept that it will be possible to fend off one of God's predicted punishments sent against a Christ rejecting world can only be seen by Bible believing Christians as futile.

Near Earth Objects Task Force Set Up

The British Department of Trade and Industries Near Earth Objects Task Force headed up by Sir Harry Atkinson, former Chairman of the European Space Agency, recently issued its report described by Sir Harry as a "Sober and scientific assessment of one of the most important risks facing mankind". The report says that the chances of a large object from space hitting the Earth and killing thousands, or even millions of people, is much higher than the public realise, and warns nations must co-operate to prevent this happening.

The report adds that any one of a hundred objects ranging from large boulders to mountain-sized lumps of rock could strike our planet without warning. Risk assessment of a Near Earth Object strike is above the line of tolerability set by the Health and Safety Executive. If this threat were the responsibility of somebody it would amount to an offence.

When an Asteroid Red Alert is Sounded.

Continuing advances in asteroid detection and tracking techniques will inevitably lead to an early warning system coming into being. Then when this alarm is sounded: "People will faint from fear as they wait for what is coming over the whole earth, for the powers in space will be driven from their courses" (Luke 21.26).

The effect upon every day life on a Satan-worshipping, unrepentant, sinful world when a warning is sounded will be electric: "Everyone who once was happy is now sad, and the joyful music of their harps and drums has ceased. There is no more happy singing over wine; no one enjoys its taste any more" (Isa. 24. 7-9).

Alien Invaders Land On Earth

One of the Bible's strangest and most mysterious predictions was given in a vision to John on the Island of Patmos. It foretells a coming invasion of earth by a massive force of alien beings of unknown origin and horrendous appearance, set on a five months mission of torture, probably just before the battle of Armageddon commences.

These invaders, John was told: "could harm only the people who did not have the mark of God's seal on their foreheads" and they "were not allowed to kill these people, but only to torture them for five months" (Rev.9. 4-5).

Huge Smoke Screen

The invasion will begin under cover of a huge smoke screen that will come down from the sky: "like the smoke from a large furnace; the sunlight and the air were darkened by the smoke" (Rev. 9.2.).

As this vast armada: "came down out of the smoke" and landed "upon the earth" (Rev. 9.3.) there came echoing out of the eerie blackness an ear shattering banging and clattering: "like the noise of many horse-drawn chariots rushing into battle" (Rev. 9.9.).

As these forces emerged into the light John saw that: "their faces were like men's faces. Their hair was like women's hair, their teeth were like lion's teeth" (Rev. 9. 7-8).

The alien's appeared to be wearing some kind of uniforms or protective clothing for: "on their heads they had what seemed to be crowns of gold" (Rev. 9.7.) and "Their chests were covered with what looked like iron breastplates" (Rev. 9.9.). They appeared to have no problem with earth's atmosphere, for there was nothing to suggest they were carrying or wearing breathing apparatus.

The instruments of torture to be employed by these invaders in their macabre mission appeared as: "tails and stings…and it is with their tails that they have power to hurt people for five months" (Rev. 9.10). The pain caused by these weapons will be: "like the pain caused by a scorpion's sting. During those five months" [the people attacked because they were without God's seal on their foreheads] "will seek death, but will not find it; they will want to die, but death will flee from them" (Rev. 9. 5-6).

These invaders, to which the name "Locusts" is given (Rev. 9.3.) were clearly not named on account of their appearance. Nor does their mission on earth resemble the natural vegetation destroying behaviour of locusts. Indeed, their instructions were: "not to harm the grass or the trees, or any other plant" (Rev. 9.4.). Rather, it seems, that the name "Locusts" may have been given to reflect the vast numbers of individuals involved in the landing, and the dogged way in which they will move over the earth in unstoppable droves similar to natural locusts. The prophet Joel also used the term "Locust" to describe the invasion of Israel in the last days: "I will remove the locust army that came from the north and will drive some of them into the desert. Their front ranks will be driven into the Dead Sea, their rear ranks into the Mediterranean. Their bodies will stink. I will destroy them because of all they have done to you." (Joel 2: 20)

A Disciplined Force

Commander of these briefed alien invaders will be their king: "They have a king ruling over them, who is the angel in charge of the abyss. His name in Hebrew is Abaddon; in Greek the name is Apollyon [meaning 'The Destroyer'] (Rev. 9.11.).

No specific timing is given in scripture for when this invasion will take place, but just prior to the beginning of the war of Armageddon seems probable.

From the Abyss

Although these invading aliens came from: "the abyss" (Rev. 9.2.), it seems unlikely that the abyss will have been their original habitation. More probably at some time in the distant past they will have been confined there as a place of punishment.

The prison role of the abyss was made clear by an angel being given: "the key of the abyss" who then "opened the abyss" (Rev. 9. 1-2).

The abyss should not be confused with Hell, for they are very different places. Hell is an awful place of torment: "day and night for ever and ever" (Rev. 20.10). A place from where there can be no release. The abyss, in contrast, is a place of imprisonment from which on Divine instructions there are releases.

Prison Role of the Abyss

Anti-Christ is at this present time, it seems, actually being held prisoner in the abyss, awaiting the time when he will be released by Divine order to: "come up out of the abyss" (Rev. 11.7.) to the earth and begin his rise to world power.

Where the abyss is situated is not revealed in scripture. However, responsible speculation would seem to point to the abyss, like the earth, and probably like heaven, being a planet or planets in God's created universe.

In the universe are an uncountable number of planets, some three hundred times larger than the earth. Scientists, using a technique called Gravitational Micro-lensing, claim to have discovered, thirty thousand light years away, another planet with a climate similar to that of the earth. Still further research is said to have resulted in the discovery of a number of other hitherto unknown planets believed to have earth-like climates.

Although there is no firm scientific evidence that any planets other than the earth are inhabited, the Bible and science both point to life on some of them being virtually certain.

That the government of the Lord Jesus extends well beyond the limits of planet earth to cover the whole universe is revealed in scripture: "God created the whole universe through him and for him", including "the seen and the unseen things, Lords, rulers and authorities" (Col. 1.16).

Life in the Universe

All life in the whole universe comes from God through the Lord Jesus: "the source of life" (John 1.4.)

Long before the world was made many millions of living personalities had been created and were living in different parts of the universe. Some of them even watched as the earth was created: "in the dawn of that day the stars [angels] sang together, and the heavenly beings shouted for joy" (Job. 38.7.).

Living in the universe are vast numbers of angels: "thousands and millions of them" (Rev. 5.11.). They have different spheres of service and hold different ranks of authority. Two thirds of them are loyal to God while the remaining third have allied themselves with Satan in rebellion against God's rule.

The Lord Jesus Christ is recorded as having visited: "above and beyond the heavens" to "fill the whole universe with his presence" (Eph. 4.10). A visit that pre-supposes life on some of the planets in these distant constellations.

An Earlier Landing

Back in the days before the flood there was an invasion of earth by human type beings from another habitation.

It was: "When mankind had spread all over the world, and girls were being born, some of the heavenly beings saw that these girls were beautiful, so they took the ones they liked. Then the Lord said, 'I will not allow people to live forever; they are mortal'...In those days, and even later, there were giants on the earth who were descendants of human women and the heavenly beings. They were the great heroes and famous men of long ago" (Gen. 6. 1-4).

These early invaders do not seem to have been angels from heaven, for Jesus said that: "the angels in heaven" do "not marry" (Matt. 22.30). They may have been the same beings referred to by

Jude: "Remember the angels who did not stay within the limits of their proper authority, but abandoned their own dwelling place" (Jude. 6.).

Space Travel

Looked at in the light of these scriptures, instant travel between far flung inhabited places in God's created universe is clearly both reported and prophesied.

Travel across the vast distances between the planets, at least in theory, is possible by teleportation. Teleportation being defined as, the instant transfer of any aggregate of matter from its present position in the universe to another place in the universe.

Physicists have believed for some years that interplanetary travel by teleportation would break no known laws of physics, though it is clear from present research levels that the obstacles to teleportation of complete macroscopic objects, for instance people, are enormous. They are however purely matters of engineering well beyond the practical abilities of man at present. Nevertheless well within the scope of God's power as the many teleportation "miracles" of the Bible show.

UFO's in our Sky

Currently from all over the world are coming reports of unidentified flying objects [UFO's] seen in the skies. Many have revealed their presence on radar screens, and some have been videoed and photographed. The origin of these UFO's or their purpose in the skies above the earth, remain a mystery. Many different theories exist about them, but so far nothing that links them with any specific Bible prophecies is known.

Armageddon Ends Man's Rule On Earth

God has revealed of the Armageddon war: "I am going to send war on all the people on earth""(Jer. 25. 29). This because: "The Lord is angry with all the nations and their armies. He has condemned them to destruction" and for this "has prepared his sword in heaven" (Isa. 34. 2.5.).

Call-up of the Demons

It seems that Satan, The World Dictator and the World Religious Primate will call up: "the spirits of demons that perform miracles" to: "go out to all the kings of the world, to bring them together for the battle on the great Day of Almighty God"(Rev.16. 13-16).

This mobilization will have taken place as a result of the World Dictator receiving intelligence reports of a huge force being gathered, and on the move towards Jerusalem from east of the River Euphrates. This river global warming will have: "dried up, to provide a way for the kings who come from the east" (Rev. 16.12).

Four Angels Released

This massive eastern force will have gathered as a result of God's instructions that: "the four angels who are bound at the great River Euphrates" should be "released... to kill a third of mankind" (Rev. 9. 14-15). This will happen only according to God's timing, for these angels are being held bound: "for this very hour of this very day of this very month and year" (Rev. 9.15.).

These four mighty but fallen angels will then provoke, deceive and incite countries east of the Euphrates into a massive battle plan against the World Dictator and his western armies occupying Israel.

History abounds with macabre acts of men incited and empowered by evil spiritual forces. Of all these the Armageddon war will be the most horrific.

The apostle Paul warns that in circumstances like these: "we are not fighting against human beings but against the wicked spiritual forces in the heavenly world, the rulers, authorities and cosmic powers of this dark age" (Eph. 6.12.).

So it will be in the war of Armageddon, though it will not look that way. For human beings will be used as pawns in the manoeuvres of the evil spiritual forces as they: "bring them [human beings] together for the battle on the great Day of Almighty God" (Rev. 16.14.).

A Two Hundred Million Strong Force

No precise details are given about which nations will contribute to this vast army, but in a vision on Patmos John saw a: "two hundred million" strong force in which "the horses and their riders... had breast plates red as fire, blue as sapphire and yellow as sulphur. The horses' heads were like lions' heads, and from their mouths came out fire, smoke, and sulphur. A third of mankind was killed by those three plagues: the fire, the smoke and the sulphur coming out of the horses' mouths. For the power of the horses is in their mouths, and in their tails" (Rev. 9. 16-19).

This horrendous prophetic picture appears to represent a modern mechanised army equipped with weapons of mass destruction. Weapons that will be used to speedily wipe out a third of the world's population.

As this gigantic invading force approaches Israel, its first objective will probably be to attack and secure control of the main Middle East oil producing centres, in an attempt to deny the western confederation armies their vital fuel supplies.

The World Dictator will speedily move his armies to confront the invaders, and the great battle of Armageddon will begin, centred around the hill of Megiddo, just west of the Jordan River and spilling out onto the surrounding plains of Esdraelon.

The vast and powerful evil forces of Satan and his angels, earlier thrown down to earth by Michael and his angels, will no doubt line up with these: "kings of the east" to fight in this great battle.

Jerusalem Captured

"Jerusalem the city that God loves" (Isa. 62.12.). Then: "the city will be taken, the houses looted, and the women raped. Half the people will go into exile, but the rest of them will not be taken away from the city" (Zech. 14. 2-3).

Jesus Appears in the Sky

These massive armies from east and west, while still locked together in desperate fighting, will suddenly become terrified and white with fear as they see a frightening sign in the sky: "Like the lightening which flashes across the whole sky from the east to the west" (Matt. 24.27), above them: "Then the sign of the Son of Man will appear in the sky; and all the peoples of earth will weep as they see the Son of Man coming on the clouds of heaven with power and great glory" (Matt. 24.30).

In the confusion and panic that follows: "everyone will seize the man next to him and attack him" (Zech. 13.14).

Suddenly, no longer will the east and west continue to fight each other, but: "together" will re-gather "to fight against... [The Lord Jesus Christ] and against his army" (Rev. 19.19).

Terrible Disease Affects Armageddon Armies.

People the world over will suffer "severe burns as the sun is: "allowed to burn people with its fiery heat." (Rev.16.8.)

At that time: "The Lord will bring a terrible disease on all the nations that make war on Jerusalem. Their flesh will rot away while they are still alive; their eyes and their tongues will rot away" (Zech. 14. 12-13).

Greatest Earthquake Ever

On that day there will be: "strange things happening to the sun, the moon and the stars" (Luke 21.25.), there will be: "flashes of lightening, rumblings and peels of thunder, and a terrible earthquake. There has never been such an earthquake since the creation of man...cities of all countries were destroyed... All the islands disappeared, [under the oceans] all the mountains vanished" [were flattened] (Rev. 16. 17-20).

People all over the world will be in a state of bewilderment that will turn into terror as: "the powers in space will be driven from their courses" (Luke 21.26). At this: "The heavens tremble, and the earth will be shaken out of its place" (Isa. 13.13.) into a changed orbit around the sun.

By this greatest earthquake of all time: "The Lord is going to devastate the earth and leave it desolate... He will twist the earth's surface and scatter its people". Then "The earth will lie shattered and ruined. The Lord has spoken and it will be done... Torrents of rain will pour from the sky, and the earth's foundation will shake. The earth will crack and shatter and split open", and will "stagger like a drunken man and sway like a hut in a storm" (Isa. 24. 1-3, 19-20).

Then: "at that time he [Jesus] will stand on the Mount of Olives, to the east of Jerusalem. Then the Mount of Olives will be split in two from east to west by a large valley. Half the mountain will move northwards and half of it southwards. You [people from Jerusalem] will escape through this valley that divides the mountain in two" (Zech. 14. 4-5).

To Isaiah concerning this time God said: "The day of the Lord is coming – that cruel day of his fierce anger and fury. The earth will be made a wilderness, and every sinner will be destroyed. Every star and every constellation will stop shining, the sun will be dark when it rises, and the moon will give no light... I will bring disaster on the earth and punish all wicked people for their sins. I will humble everyone who is proud and punish everyone who is arrogant and cruel." (Isa.13.9-12)

Human Pride Ended

Then on earth: "human pride will be ended and human arrogance will be destroyed... the Lord alone will be exalted on that day. People will hide in caves in the rocky hills or dig holes in the ground to try to escape from the Lord's anger and hide from his power and glory, when he comes to shake the earth" (Isa. 2. 17-19).

So wicked will mankind have become that no longer will God allow them to rule on the earth, and as from the clouds he descends Jesus will by his word of command destroy all the armies engaged in the Armageddon war. The World Dictator, and the Religious Primate will be taken prisoners: "The Lord will punish the powers above and the rulers of the earth [World Dictator and Religious Primate]... he will shut them in prison until the time of their punishment comes" (Isa. 24. 21-22).

Satan Imprisoned

Satan will be arrested as John saw in a vision an angel: "seized the dragon, that ancient serpent that is, the Devil... and chained him up for a thousand years" (Rev. 20.2.).

Regeneration of the World

After Armageddon: "The earth will lie shattered and ruined." (Isa. 24. 3.) It seems likely that only one quarter to one third of the earth's population will remain alive.

The Lord Jesus Christ, his victory over the Armageddon armies completed, will set up his: "rule over the nations" (Isa. 51.5.). He will establish at Jerusalem: "the Throne of the Lord" (Jer. 3.17) and fulfil the promise given to his apostles by the angels at his ascension: "Jesus... will come back in the same way that you saw him go to heaven" (Acts 1.11).

At that time Jesus: "will be king over all the earth and everybody will know him by the same name" (Zech. 14.9.).

The Same Jesus

Jesus will return to earth at this time in his resurrection body. The same body in which during the forty days between his resurrection and ascension he: "appeared... many times in ways that prove beyond doubt that he was alive" (Acts 1.3.). He: "ate and drank" (Acts 10.41) with his followers and frequently spent time with them and: "talked with them" (Acts. 1.3.).

On one occasion he told them: "look at my hands and my feet, and see that it is I myself. Feel me, and you will know, for a ghost doesn't have flesh and bones [no mention of blood] as you can see I have... he asked them, have you anything here to eat? They gave him a piece of cooked fish, which he took and ate in their presence" (Luke 24. 39-43).

The Angels Come with Jesus

The Lord Jesus when he comes to reign will be: "bringing all the angels with him" (Zech. 14.5.), angels who will probably have the appearance of men.

Back in Old Testament times when two angels accompanied the Lord on his visit to Abraham they looked, walked and spoke like men and when Abraham offered them: "some cream, some milk and the meat... they ate" (Gen. 18.8.).

When the angel Gabriel came to explain to Daniel the meaning of his visions Gabriel too: "looked like a man" (Dan. 10.16).

Much later, at the time of Jesus' ascension, two angels appeared and spoke to the apostles, who saw them as: "two men dressed in white" that: "suddenly stood beside them" (Acts. 1.10).

Resurrection and Changed Christian Believers come with Jesus

As well as being accompanied at his second coming by angels, Jesus will also bring with him then those Christian believers whom he will have gathered up into heaven from earth when on an earlier occasion he will have: "come down from heaven...in the clouds" (1 Thess. 4. 16-17), this: "not to deal with sin but to save those who are waiting for him" (Heb. 9.28).

Then while up in heaven before returning to earth with the Lord Jesus, these: "rescued" ones will have received an "immortal... beautiful and strong... spiritual body" (1 Cor. 15. 42-44), a body of spiritual flesh and bones: "to be like him" (1 John 3.2.). At the same time they will have been endowed with knowledge that: "will be complete" (1 Cor. 13.12.). Ready: "to share his glory" (Heb. 2.10), and in union with Jesus: "to judge the world" (1 Cor. 6.2.)

Tribulation Martyrs Resurrected

John on Patmos saw in a vision that resurrected at about this time will be: "those who had been executed (during the three and a half years of great tribulation) because they had proclaimed the truth that Jesus revealed and the word of God. They had not worshipped the beast or his image, nor had they received the mark of the beast on their foreheads or their hands. They came to life and ruled as kings with Christ for a thousand years" (Rev. 20.4.)

Under the jurisdiction of these "kings" will be the "nations' leaders" who will then "govern with justice", with "their eyes and ears… open to the needs of the people… they will act with understanding and will say what they mean" (Isa. 32.1. & 3-4).

Resurrection and Judgement of Israel's Dead

It will probably be about this time that there will be a resurrection and judgement for the people of Israel who have died earlier: "When that time comes, all the people of your nation [Israel] whose names are written in God's book will be saved. Many of those who have already died will live again; some will enjoy eternal life, and some will suffer eternal disgrace. The wise leaders will shine with all the brightness of the sky. And those who have taught many people to do what is right will shine like the stars for ever" (Dan. 12. 1-3). The prophet Isaiah reveals of these Jewish people: "their bodies will come back to life. All those sleeping in the graves will wake up and sing for joy. As the sparkling dew refreshes the earth, so the Lord will revive those who have long been dead" (Isa. 26.19).

Israel Tested

From his throne in Jerusalem the Lord Jesus will then address the living among God's chosen people Israel warning them: "I will show you my power and my anger when I gather you together and bring you back from all the countries where you have been scattered. I will bring you into the 'Desert of the Nations', and there I will condemn you to your face… I will take firm control of you and make you obey my covenant. I will take away from among you those who are rebellious and sinful. I will take them out of the lands where they are living now, but I will not let them return to the land of Israel. Then you will know that I am the Lord'" (Ezek. 20. 34-38)

Israel Filled with the Spirit

At this time: "Two thirds of the people [of Israel] will die" and God further warns: "I will test the third that survive and will purify them as silver is purified by fire. I will test them as gold is tested. Then they will pray to me and I will answer them, I will tell them that they are my people, and they will confess that I am their God" (Zech. 13. 8-9)

To the surviving third who are allowed back to live in their promised land God says: "I will use you to show the nations that I am holy... I will sprinkle clean water on you and make you clean from all your idols and everything else that has defiled you. I will give you a new heart and a new mind. I will take away your stubborn heart of stone and give you an obedient heart. I will put my spirit in you and I will see to it that you follow my laws and keep all the commands I have given you. Then... you will be my people and I will be your God'" (Ezek. 36. 23 & 25-28). Then: "everyone who is left in Jerusalem, whom God has chosen for survival, will be called holy" (Isa. 4.3.).

Chosen to personally rule with Jesus in Jerusalem at that time will be the twelve apostles to whom Jesus promised: "you who have followed Me, in the regeneration when the Son of Man will sit on His glorious Throne, you also shall sit upon twelve thrones, judging the twelve tribes of Israel" (Matt. 19.28) New American Standard).

All Evil to be Removed from Earth

Before Jesus begins his reign as king over all the earth however there will be the rooting out of remaining evil from wherever it is to be found, for: "The Lord does not easily become angry, but he is powerful and never lets the guilty go unpunished" (Nahum. 1.3.). So: "By fire and sword he will punish all the people of the world whom he finds guilty and many will be put to death" (Isa. 66. 15.-16): "Those who survive will be scarcer than gold" (Isa. 13.12.)

At this judgement the Lord Jesus: "will sit on his royal throne, and the people of all the nations will be gathered before him. Then he will divide them into two groups... He will put the righteous people on his right and the others on his left. Then the King will say to the people on his right: 'Come, you that are blessed by my Father! Come and possess the kingdom which has been prepared for you ever since the creation of the world'... Then he will say to those on his left, 'away from me, you that are under God's curse!" (Matt. 25. 31-34 & 41).

To understand the logistics of this event calls for recognition of Jesus' divine ability to work in the spiritual dimension, a dimension that can never be fully understood by finite minds. For when: "the people of all nations will be gathered before him" (Matt. 25. 32), it will be no more necessary for Jesus in person to travel to all parts of the world to judge them than it was for him to travel the world in order to see before him: "all the kingdoms of the world in all their greatness" (Matt. 4.8.) from the very high mountain to which Satan had taken him at the time of his temptation in the wilderness.

The carrying out of capital punishment on those found guilty by the Lord might be seen as not unlike the time when: "at midnight the Lord killed all the first-born sons in Egypt, from the king's son, who was heir to the throne, to the son of the prisoner in the dungeon." (Exod. 12.29) This when the Egyptians refused to release the Israelites from their slavery.

After the Lord Jesus' judgements have been made it will be a time of euphoria, and "those who survive will sing for joy. Those in the west will tell how great the Lord is, and those in the east will praise him. The people who live along the sea will praise the Lord, the God of Israel" (Isa. 24. 14-15).

Theocratic Rule from Jerusalem.

With his theocratic governmental arrangements in place: "Over Mount Zion and all that are gathered there, the Lord will send a cloud in the daytime and smoke and a bright flame at night. God's glory will cover and protect the whole city" (Isa. 4.5.). This is reminiscent of the time when, after their escape from slavery in Egypt the Israelites spent forty years in the desert:

"During all their wanderings they could see the cloud of the Lord's presence over the tent (the tabernacle containing the altar of the Lord) during the day and a fire burning above it during the night" (Exo. 40.38).

Jesus: King Over All the Earth

When Jesus is king over all the earth and with his theocratic governmental arrangements in place, those found faithful to remain to possess the kingdom will live to enjoy long lives indeed: "Those who live to be a hundred will be considered young. To die before that would be a sign that I had punished them. People will build houses and live in them themselves – they will not be used by someone else. They will plant vineyards and enjoy the wine – it will not be drunk by others. They will fully enjoy the things that they have worked for." (Isa. 65. 20-22)

Filled with the love and power of the Holy Spirit the people of Israel will embark on their role as priests to the nations of the world: "The people of Israel who survive will be like refreshing dew sent by the Lord for many nations, like showers on growing plants. They will depend on God, not man" (Mica. 5.7.). And: "In those days ten foreigners will come to one Jew and say, "We want to share in your destiny, because we have heard that God is with you" (Zech. 8.23).

Of the Israelis at that time God says: "They will be famous among the nations; everyone who sees them will know that they are a people whom I have blessed" (Isa. 61.9.).

Because of their ministry among the nations they: "will be known as the priests of the Lord, the servants of our God" (Isa. 61.6.). This ministry was foreshadowed when just after Pentecost: "Many miracles and wonders were being performed among the people by the apostles...crowds of people came in from the towns around Jerusalem, bringing those who were ill or who had evil spirits in them; and they were all healed" (Acts. 5. 12 & 16). The writer to the Hebrews comments of these people that they had: "felt the powers of the coming age" (Heb. 6.5.).

Right living will be practised everywhere by the Israelis: "The people of Israel who survive will do no wrong to anyone, tell no lies, nor try to deceive" (Zeph. 3.13.), and to them God has promised: "even before they finish praying to me I will answer their prayers" (Isa. 65.24.).

Topographical Changes in the Land of Israel

As the Lord Jesus will make his royal descent from heaven to the Mount of Olives so, by means of a massive earthquake, God will redesign the countryside around Jerusalem. This to fit that city to fulfil its prestigious role of world capital: "Then the Mount of Olives will be split in two from east to west by a large valley. Half the mountain will move northwards and half of it southwards... when that day comes, fresh water will flow from Jerusalem, half of it to the Dead Sea and the other half to the Mediterranean. It will flow all the year round, in the dry season as well as the wet. The whole region, from Geba in the north to Rimmon in the south will be made level. Jerusalem will tower above the land round it" (Zech. 14. 4. 8-10).

Then: "Over Mount Zion and all that are gathered there, the Lord will send a cloud in the daytime and smoke and a bright flame at night. God's glory will cover and protect the whole city" (Isa. 4.5.). This is reminiscent of the time when, after their escape from slavery in Egypt the Israelites spent forty years in the desert: "During all their wanderings they could see the cloud of the Lord's presence over the tent (the tabernacle containing the altar of the Lord) during the day and a fire burning above it during the night" (Exo. 40.38).

This violent earthquake will create a massive inland waterway so that Isaiah was able to prophecy about the inhabitants of Jerusalem at that time: "we will live beside broad rivers and streams, but hostile ships will not sail on them" (Isa. 33.21.).

Probably this broad river and lake system will carry passenger and cargo shipping from ports all over the world to dock at Jerusalem: "the wealth of the nations will be brought to you; from across the seas these riches will come" (Isa. 60.5).

The other significant topographical redesign in the area will result in the whole of Geba in the north to Rimmon in the south becoming an ideal site for building the worlds largest and finest airports. Prompting Isaiah to predict air travel several thousand years before the first aircraft ever flew: "What are these ships that skim along like clouds, like doves returning home? They are ships coming from distant lands, bringing God's people home. They bring with them silver and gold to honour the name of the Lord, the holy God of Israel, who has made all nations honour his people" (Isa. 60.8-9).

The Hub of World Transport

Together these two great God provided changes in the Jerusalem landscape will make the city the hub of world transport: "Look at Jerusalem" God declares, "I put her at the centre of the world, with other countries all round her" (Ezek. 5.5.). Strategically placed: "at the cross-roads of the world" (Ezek. 38.12). Israel will then be built up by God to become the greatest nation the world has ever known: "Once again I will rebuild you. Once again you will take up your tambourines and dance joyfully... the Lord says 'sing with joy for Israel the greatest of all the nations'" (Jer. 31. 4 & 7).

The wealth of Israel at that time will become immense: "I will bring you lasting prosperity; the wealth of the nations will flow to you like a river that never goes dry" (Isa. 66.12.).

The other nations will be amazed as they witness this plan of God's developing: "every nation in the world will fear and tremble when they hear about the good things that I do for the people of Jerusalem and about the prosperity that I bring to the city" (Jer. 33.9.). Then visitors arriving at Jerusalem by air, sea or land will be awe-struck by the sight of that magnificent city built on a hill, towering above all the land around it and visibly covered by God's protecting presence by cloud and flame.

New Temple Built to God's Plans

During the early part of Jesus' millennial reign a new Temple will be built on the summit of Mount Zion. Built to God's own plans: "the Lord will make his Temple more glorious than ever" (Isa. 60.7.), Then: "all the area surrounding it on the top of the mountain" God has decreed will be: "Sacred and Holy" (Ezek. 43.12.).

Even the animal kingdom will be radically changed in nature: "Wolves and sheep will live together in peace and leopards will lie down with young goats. Calves and lion cubs will feed together, and little children will take care of them. Cows and bears will eat together, and their calves and cubs will lie down in peace. Lions will eat straw as cattle do. Even a baby will not be harmed if it plays near a poisonous snake. On Zion, God's sacred hill there will be nothing harmful or evil" (Isa. 11. 6-9).

This sacred mountain top area: "is to be twelve and a half kilometres long by ten kilometres wide"(Ezek. 45.1.), half of it is to be used for the Temple building and its immediate surrounding land, and: "The other half of the area is to be set aside as the possession of the Levites, who do the work in the Temple. There will be towns there for them to live in" (Ezek. 45.5.).

In this new Temple there is to be a return to animal sacrifices. These sacrifices to be offered only by: "Those priests belonging to the tribe of Levi who are descended from Zadok" (Ezek. 44.15.), who himself was descended from Aaron the first high priest.

The President of the State of Israel will at that time combine his Presidential role with the office of Chief Executive of the Temple, and when invited, God says this VIP: "may go there [into the Temple] to eat a holy meal in my presence" (Ezek. 44.3.)

Temple Worship for Gentiles as well as Jews

At that time worship in the newly built Temple will be opened up to Gentiles as well as Jews. Then, God says: "I will change the people of the nations, and they will pray to me alone and not to other gods. They will all obey me" (Zeph. 3.9.). Also, the Lord says to: "those foreigners who have become part of his people, who love him and serve him, who observe the Sabbath and faithfully keep his covenant, "I will bring you to Zion, my sacred hill, give you joy in my house of prayer, and accept the sacrifices you offer on my altar. My Temple will be called a house of prayer for the people of all nations" (Isa. 56.6.).

From then onwards people of all nations will travel to Jerusalem to visit the Temple, and find out God's will for their lives: "Many nations... will say, "let us go up to the hill of the Lord, to the Temple of Israel's God. He will teach us what he wants us to do; we will walk in the paths he has chosen. For the Lord's teaching comes from Jerusalem, from Zion he speaks to his people" (Isa. 2. 2-3). These worshippers made up of: "many people and powerful nations will come to Jerusalem to worship the Lord Almighty, and to pray for his blessing" (Zech. 8.22.).

In addition to those who desire to go to the Temple to worship God and learn from him there will be a requirement that all the nations who have been involved in the battle of Armageddon send representatives annually to the Festival of Shelters. "Then all the survivors from the nations that have attacked Jerusalem will go there each year to worship the Lord Almighty as king... if any nation refuses... then rain will not fall on their land" (Zech. 14. 16-17).

God's Own Presence

To Ezekiel God revealed that his presence would be found within the new Temple: "I saw coming from the east the dazzling light of the presence of the God of Israel... the dazzling light passed through the east gate and went into the Temple... I saw that the Temple was filled with the glory of the Lord... I heard the Lord speak to me out of the Temple: Mortal man here is my throne. I will live here among the people of Israel and rule over them for ever" (Ezek. 43. 2 &4-7).

Some idea of what it may be like to worship God in this new Temple may be gained from the account of an actual experience in the original Temple at Jerusalem during King Solomon's reign: "The dazzling light of the Lord's presence filled the Temple. Because the

Temple was full of the dazzling light the priests could not enter it", then "the people of Israel... fell face downwards on the pavement worshipping God and praising him" (2 Chron. 7. 1-3).

Although vast numbers of people from around the world will travel to Jerusalem to worship God in his Temple, not everyone will find it possible to do so. For them there will be a place of worship locally: "People from one end of the world to the other honour me. Everywhere they burn incense to me and offer acceptable sacrifices. All of them honour me!" (Mal. 1.11).

An Altar to the Lord in Egypt

For forty years after Armageddon Egypt will have been an empty waste. It's people gone, and the land so heavily contaminated that: "no human being or animal will walk through it" (Ezek. 29. 11) and: "When that time comes, there will be an altar to the Lord in the land of Egypt and a stone pillar dedicated to him at the Egyptian border. They will be symbols of the Lord Almighty's presence in Egypt"... Then "The Lord will reveal himself to the Egyptian people, and they will acknowledge and worship him, and bring him sacrifices and offerings"... Then "they [the Egyptians] will turn to him [God] and he will hear their prayers and heal them" (Isa. 19.19-22),

Arabs and Jews Together Bless the Nations

Israel will then no longer be alone in blessing all the nations. For: "when that time comes, there will be a highway between Egypt and Assyria. The people of these two countries will travel to and fro between them, and the two nations will worship together. When that time comes, Israel will rank with Egypt and Assyria, and these three nations will be a blessing to the world" (Isa. 19. 23-24).

From among the nations at this time there will be some who go to live in the land of Israel: "One by one, people will say, 'I am the Lord's'. They will come to join the people of Israel. Each one will mark the name of the Lord on his arm and call himself one of God's people" (Isa. 44.5.).

A River Will Flow from the Temple

In Ezekiel's vision of the millennial Temple he saw that: "water was coming out from under the entrance... of the Temple... five hundred metres downstream... the water came only to my ankles... another five hundred metres, and the water came up to my knees... another five hundred metres further down the water was up to my waist... five hundred metres more and there the stream was so deep I could not wade through it... this water flows through the land to the east, and down to the Jordan Valley and to the Dead Sea. When it flows into the Dead Sea it replaces the salt water of that sea with fresh water... there will be as many different kinds of fish there as there are in the Mediterranean Sea" (Ezek. 47. 1-10).

To the prophet Joel this coming water supply was also revealed, enabling him to predict: "there will be plenty of water for all the streams of Judah. A stream will flow from the Temple of the Lord, and it will water the Valley of Acacia" (Joel. 3.18).

No Sickness in Israel

Amazingly, in the land of Israel at this time, sickness will be unknown: "No one who lives in our land will ever again complain of being ill, and all sins will be forgiven" (Isa. 33.24.). Then: "the blind will be able to see, and the deaf hear. The lame will leap and dance, and those who cannot speak will shout for joy... they will be happy for ever, for ever free from sorrow and grief" (Isa. 35. 5-6 & 10) and amidst this blessing: "the girls will dance and be happy, and men, young and old will rejoice" (Jer. 31.13.).

Not surprisingly people will live longer lives: "Babies will no longer die in infancy, and all people will live out their life span. Those who live to be a hundred will be considered young. To die before that would be a sign that I have punished them...like trees, my people will live long lives" (Isa. 65. 20-23), as they did from the beginning of the Genesis creation until the time of the flood. Then it was not unusual to live to be eight hundred to nine hundred years old, sometimes a little older. Adam for instance lived to be nine hundred and thirty, his son Seth to be nine hundred and twelve and his son Enoch to be nine hundred and five.

Crops Grow Faster than can be Harvested.

In the land of Israel then, all of nature will reflect God's goodness to his people: "The Lord will make every plant and tree in the land grow large and beautiful. All the people of Israel who survive will take delight and pride in the crops that the land produces". (Isa. 4.2.)

The harvests then will be bountiful beyond human understanding, for: "corn will grow faster that it can be harvested, and grapes will grow faster than the wine can be made." (Amos. 9.13)

Earth Shaken into New Orbit Round Sun.

Mega abundance in nature is likely to be brought about by a sudden change in climate from the searing heat of the final phase of global warming into a perfect climate for growing when the earth is: "shaken out of its place" (Isa. 13.13.), into a new orbital path around the sun. Then: "There will no longer be any cold or frost, nor any darkness. There will always be daylight, even at night time" (Zech. 14. 6-7).

Large areas of currently unproductive desert and wilderness, such as the Sahara and Antarctica, will become rich and fertile land. For then: "streams of water will flow through the desert; the burning sand will become a lake, and dry land will be filled with springs" (Isa. 35. 6-7).

Then: "flowers will bloom in the wilderness. The desert... will be as beautiful as the Lebanon Mountains and as fertile as the fields of Carmel" (Isa. 35. 1`-2) and: "forests will grow in barren land, forests of pine, and juniper and cypress" (Isa. 41.19).

A team of scientists at the Hebrew University in Jerusalem has recently discovered a growth gene which when introduced to trees fruit and vegetables can allow them to grow thirty to fifty per cent faster. The implications of this discovery when the time arrives for the planting of these regenerated and re-claimed deserts and wildernesses will be immense.

Prosperous Industries

Not only agriculture but industry too will prosper and flourish under the Lord Jesus' kingdom rule. There will be plenty, and it will be fairly distributed amongst all the nations.

Through his rule from Jerusalem, Jesus: "will settle disputes among great nations who will hammer their swords into ploughs and their spears into pruning knives. Nations will never again go to war, never prepare for battle again" (Isa. 2.4.).

Massive defence budgets will no longer be needed, leaving vast sums of money available for more constructive purposes.

Human Sin Persists

During Satan's one thousand years imprisonment many millions of children will have been born and will have grown up on the earth. Although born into a kingdom of justice and peace some, perhaps many of them, will: "never learn to do what is right. Even here in a land of righteous people they still do wrong" (Isa. 26.10).

Then: "After the thousand years are over, Satan will be let loose from his prison" for a little while, "and he will go out to deceive the nations scattered over the whole world" (Rev. 20.7.).

Probably one of the first deceits that Satan will successfully bring upon the nations after his release will be to urge them to restart their armament industries once again.

Earth's Final Battle

Satan has again tricked the nations into enlisting and equipping their armies, human and evil spiritual forces will unite at this time: "all the nations of the world will join forces to attack her" [Jerusalem]. He: "will bring them all together for battle... they spread out over the earth and surrounded the camp of God's people [Israel] and the city that he loves. But fire came down from heaven and destroyed them" (Rev. 20. 8-9).

To the people of Israel at this time the divine promise is: "Suddenly and unexpectedly the Lord Almighty will rescue you with violent thunder storms and earthquakes. He will send tempests and raging fire; then all the armies of the nations attacking the city of God's altar, all their weapons and equipment – everything – will vanish like a dream, like something imagined in the night" (Isa. 29. 5-7). For: "On that day they will burn up, and there will be nothing left of them." (Mal. 4.1.)

After that: "the Devil, who deceived them was thrown into the lake of fire and sulphur, where the beast [the tyrannical world dictator] and the false prophet [the apostate world religious leader] had already been thrown" (Rev. 20.10).

New Heavens and New Earth

At that time: "the heavens will disappear with a shrill noise, the heavenly bodies will burn up and be destroyed, and the earth with everything in it will vanish" (2 Peter 3.10).

Then all those found worthy go on to inherit: "what God has promised; new heavens and a new earth, where righteousness will be at home" (2 Peter 3.13.).

A
DIVINE INVITATION

"Turn to me now and be saved,
people all over the world!
I am the only God there is"

(Isa. 45.22)

"The Lord...does not want anyone
to be destroyed, but wants all to turn away
from their sins".

(2 Peter 3:9)

Jesus says... "I am the way,
the truth, and the life;
no one goes to the Father
except by me".

(John 14.6.)

"Everyone has sinned and is far away
from God's saving presence".

(Rom. 3.23)

"God has shown us how much he loves us-it is
while we were still sinners that Christ died for us!
By his sacrificial death we are now put
right with God; how much more, then, will we be
saved by him from God's anger!"

(Rom. 5. 8-9)

"If you confess that Jesus is Lord and
believe that God raised him from death,
you will be saved".

(Rom. 10.9)

"Whoever believes in the Son is not judged;
but whoever does not believe has already
been judged, because he has not believed
in God's only Son".

(John 3.18)

"Serve the true and living God and...wait for
his Son to come from heaven – his Son
Jesus whom he raised from death and who
rescues us from God's anger that is coming."

(1 Thess 1. 9-10)

Jesus said…
"The sky and the earth won't last
forever, but my words will".
(Luke 21.33. CEV)

APPENDIX

Citizens of Heaven

In this appendix we look back to the Divine lifting of all believing Christians from earth into heaven, and at the amazing events that follow in heaven.

Only with enlightenment by the Holy Spirit does it become possible to grasp the magnitude of the glories awaiting all Christian believers as "Citizens of Heaven." (Phil. 3:20)

Something the apostle Paul recognized when he said: "we speak, not in words taught us by human wisdom but in words taught by the Spirit, expressing spiritual truths in spiritual words. The man without the Spirit does not accept the things that come from the Spirit of God, for they are foolishness to him, and he cannot understand them, because they are spiritually discerned." (1 Cor. 2. 13-14 NIV)

The promise from God for all Christian believers is that he: "Did not choose us to suffer his anger...but died for us in order that we might live together with him, whether we are alive or dead when he comes." (1 Thess. 5. 9-10)

The apostle Paul shares with us an enthralling secret: "Listen to this secret truth" he says, "we shall not all die, but when the last trumpet sounds, we shall all be changed in an instant, as quickly as the blinking of an eye. For when the trumpet sounds, the dead will be raised, never to die again, and we shall all be changed... into what is immortal...so when this takes place...death is destroyed; victory is complete!" (1 Cor. 15. 51-54)

As we have already seen earlier in this handbook the apostle Paul gives a vivid prophetic account of how this awesome transfer of Christians from earth to heaven will be: "The Lord himself will come down from heaven. Those who have died believing in Christ will rise to life first; then we who are living at that time will be gathered up along with them in the clouds to meet the Lord in the air." (1 Thess. 4. 16-17)

Prepared for Heaven

The experience of death, or of being gathered up into heaven alive when Jesus appears the second time can be faced with complete confidence because: "God is the one who has prepared us for this change." (2 Cor. 5.5.)

Not only are we already prepared for this change from earthly to heavenly life but additionally we have been given a Divine assurance: "The truth is that Christ has been raised from death, as the guarantee that those who sleep in death can also be raised." (1 Cor. 15.20)

Furthermore, what a confidence builder it is to know: "how very great is his power at work in us who believe. This power working in us is the same as the mighty strength which he used when he raised Christ...and seated him at his right side in the heavenly world." (Eph. 1. 19-20)

Heavenly Praise

In a vision of heaven given to John while a prisoner on the Island of Patmos he saw: "There in heaven was a throne with someone sitting on it. His faced gleamed" and "all round the throne there was a rainbow the colour of an emerald." Praise and worship towards the one on the throne continues day and night with Celestial voices singing the words: "Holy, holy, holy is the Lord God Almighty who was, who is, and who is to come." (Rev. 4. 1-8)

Every Spiritual Blessing

What it will be like to suddenly discover ourselves in heaven outstretches the limits of human grasp! For although God has already: "blessed us by giving us every spiritual blessing in the heavenly world" (Eph. 1.3.) it will not be until we arrive in heaven that we shall be able to appropriate them. Until that time arrives we have been told to: "look forward to possessing the rich blessings that God keeps for his people. He keeps them for you in heaven, where they cannot decay or spoil or fade away." (1 Peter 1.4.)

We Shall be Like Jesus

One of God's most gracious mega promises to believing Christians as his: "sons and daughters" (2 Cor. 6-18) is that once in heaven: "we will wear the likeness of the Man from heaven." (1 Cor. 15.49)

This Christ like body: "will be immortal...beautiful and strong...a spiritual body." (1 Cor. 15.42-44) Not ghostlike but of spiritual: "flesh and bones" (no mention of blood). (Luke 24. 39)

Not only are we to have an immortal body of great beauty and strength but also a mind possessing complete knowledge: "Now I know in part (imperfectly), but then I shall understand fully and clearly, even in the same manner as I have been fully and clearly known and understood [by God]." (1 Cor. 13.12. Amplified Bible)

A Judgement of Believers Service

Probably there will be an early appointment in heaven to stand before the Lord Jesus for: "all of us must appear before Christ, to be judged by him. Each one will receive what he deserves, according to everything he has done, good or bad, in his bodily life." (2 Cor. 5.10) This will not be a judgement of believers themselves but of their Christian service.

Speaking about this judgement Paul says: "The quality of each person's work will be seen when the Day of Christ exposes it. For on that Day fire will reveal everyone's work; the fire will test it and show its real quality. If what was built on the foundation survives the fire, the builder will receive a reward. But if anyone's work is burnt up, then he will lose it; but he himself will be saved, as if he had escaped through the fire." (1 Cor. 3. 13-15)

The verdict of this testing of believers earthly service will not be summed up by a verdict of guilty or not guilty as in a court of law, but by the awarding or withholding of rewards.

Whilst our salvation is secure for always, kept safe by the power of Jesus' sacrifice on the cross, our rewards may be lost through our own waywardness, so: "Be on your guard, then, so that you will not lose what you have worked for, but will receive your reward in full." (2 John 8.)

God has promised that not only will he reward believers for their Christian service but also for the example they set in their secular employment: "Whatever you do, work at it with all your heart, as though you were working for the Lord and not for men. Remember that the Lord will give you as a reward what he has kept for his people. For Christ is the real Master you serve." (Col. 3. 23.24)

The apostle Peter adds the important dimension of motive urging: "Do your work, not for mere pay, but from a real desire to serve...And when the Chief Shepherd appears, you will receive the glorious crown which will never lose its brightness." (1 Peter 5. 2-4)

Adoption into Heavenly Responsibilities

Before being called upon to rule with Jesus: "in the heavenly world" (Eph. 2.6.), to "judge the world" and to "judge the angels" (1 Cor. 6. 2-3), will come the time of our adoption. The apostle Paul says we are: "to wait eagerly for our adoption as sons (and daughters)" (Rom. 8. 23. NIV)

Adoption is the act of God, whereby one already a child of God is placed in the position of an adult son or daughter. It is the time that we are promoted into ruling responsibilities, ready to begin reigning with the Lord Jesus Christ.

It will be at this time that we, already in our immortal bodies and possessing complete knowledge will be displayed by God to all creation as his new ruling family. Until that time: "all of creation waits with eager longing for God to reveal his sons" (Rom. 8.19).

The Lord Jesus Christ, elder brother of all God's children, has already gone before his younger brothers and sisters through resurrection and has begun to rule: "Our Lord Jesus Christ: as to his humanity, he was born a descendant of David; as to his divine holiness, he was shown with great power to be the Son of God by being raised from death." (Rom. 1. 3-4)

Sharing the Glory of Jesus

The Lord Jesus Christ died on the cross "to bring many sons to share his glory. For Jesus is the one who leads them to salvation...He and those who are made pure all have the same Father. That is why Jesus is not ashamed to call them his brothers," (Heb. 2. 10-11) for: "Those whom God had already chosen he also set apart to become like his Son, so that the Son would be the first among many brothers." (Rom. 8.29)

Amazingly the apostle Paul reveals of Jesus' second coming: "When he appears you too will appear with him and share his glory." (Col. 3.4.)

The apostle Peter also confirms this great heavenly future for us as believing Christians: "you will receive praise and glory and honour on the Day when Jesus Christ is revealed." (1 Peter 1.7.)

Later, Peter goes on to announce how great and wonderful is the promise that: "The God of all grace...calls you to share his eternal glory in union with Christ." (1 Peter 5.10)

We can be fully assured, with this exalted family role ahead of us that God will provide the full range of abilities needed for these truly awesome responsibilities to be fully and honourably carried out.